HowExpert Guide to Native American Beadwork

80 Tips to Learn about the Art and Love of Creating Your Own Native American Beadwork

HowExpert with Leonora Raye

Copyright HowExpert™
<u>www.HowExpert.com</u>

For more tips related to this topic, visit <u>HowExpert.com/nativebeadwork</u>

Recommended Resources

- HowExpert.com – Quick 'How To' Guides on All Topics from A to Z by Everyday Experts.
- HowExpert.com/free – Free HowExpert Email Newsletter.
- HowExpert.com/books – HowExpert Books
- HowExpert.com/courses – HowExpert Courses
- HowExpert.com/clothing – HowExpert Clothing
- HowExpert.com/membership – HowExpert Membership Site
- HowExpert.com/affiliates – HowExpert Affiliate Program
- HowExpert.com/jobs – HowExpert Jobs
- HowExpert.com/writers – Write About Your #1 Passion/Knowledge/Expertise & Become a HowExpert Author.
- HowExpert.com/resources – Additional HowExpert Recommended Resources
- YouTube.com/HowExpert – Subscribe to HowExpert YouTube.
- Instagram.com/HowExpert – Follow HowExpert on Instagram.
- Facebook.com/HowExpert – Follow HowExpert on Facebook.
- TikTok.com/@HowExpert – Follow HowExpert on TikTok.

Publisher's Foreword

Dear HowExpert Reader,

HowExpert publishes quick 'how to' guides on all topics from A to Z by everyday experts.

At HowExpert, our mission is to discover, empower, and maximize everyday people's talents to ultimately make a positive impact in the world for all topics from A to Z...one everyday expert at a time!

All of our HowExpert guides are written by everyday people just like you and me, who have a passion, knowledge, and expertise for a specific topic.

We take great pride in selecting everyday experts who have a passion, real-life experience in a topic, and excellent writing skills to teach you about the topic you are also passionate about and eager to learn.

We hope you get a lot of value from our HowExpert guides, and it can make a positive impact on your life in some way. All of our readers, including you, help us continue living our mission of positively impacting the world for all spheres of influences from A to Z.

If you enjoyed one of our HowExpert guides, then please take a moment to send us your feedback from wherever you got this book.

Thank you, and we wish you all the best in all aspects of life.

Sincerely,

BJ Min
Founder & Publisher of HowExpert
HowExpert.com

PS...If you are also interested in becoming a HowExpert author, then please visit our website at HowExpert.com/writers. Thank you & again, all the best!

COPYRIGHT, LEGAL NOTICE AND DISCLAIMER:

COPYRIGHT © BY HOWEXPERT™ (OWNED BY HOT METHODS). ALL RIGHTS RESERVED WORLDWIDE. NO PART OF THIS PUBLICATION MAY BE REPRODUCED IN ANY FORM OR BY ANY MEANS, INCLUDING SCANNING, PHOTOCOPYING, OR OTHERWISE WITHOUT PRIOR WRITTEN PERMISSION OF THE COPYRIGHT HOLDER.

DISCLAIMER AND TERMS OF USE: PLEASE NOTE THAT MUCH OF THIS PUBLICATION IS BASED ON PERSONAL EXPERIENCE AND ANECDOTAL EVIDENCE. ALTHOUGH THE AUTHOR AND PUBLISHER HAVE MADE EVERY REASONABLE ATTEMPT TO ACHIEVE COMPLETE ACCURACY OF THE CONTENT IN THIS GUIDE, THEY ASSUME NO RESPONSIBILITY FOR ERRORS OR OMISSIONS. ALSO, YOU SHOULD USE THIS INFORMATION AS YOU SEE FIT, AND AT YOUR OWN RISK. YOUR PARTICULAR SITUATION MAY NOT BE EXACTLY SUITED TO THE EXAMPLES ILLUSTRATED HERE; IN FACT, IT'S LIKELY THAT THEY WON'T BE THE SAME, AND YOU SHOULD ADJUST YOUR USE OF THE INFORMATION AND RECOMMENDATIONS ACCORDINGLY.

THE AUTHOR AND PUBLISHER DO NOT WARRANT THE PERFORMANCE, EFFECTIVENESS OR APPLICABILITY OF ANY SITES LISTED OR LINKED TO IN THIS BOOK. ALL LINKS ARE FOR INFORMATION PURPOSES ONLY AND ARE NOT WARRANTED FOR CONTENT, ACCURACY OR ANY OTHER IMPLIED OR EXPLICIT PURPOSE.

ANY TRADEMARKS, SERVICE MARKS, PRODUCT NAMES OR NAMED FEATURES ARE ASSUMED TO BE THE PROPERTY OF THEIR RESPECTIVE OWNERS, AND ARE USED ONLY FOR REFERENCE. THERE IS NO IMPLIED ENDORSEMENT IF WE USE ONE OF THESE TERMS.

NO PART OF THIS BOOK MAY BE REPRODUCED, STORED IN A RETRIEVAL SYSTEM, OR TRANSMITTED BY ANY OTHER MEANS: ELECTRONIC, MECHANICAL, PHOTOCOPYING, RECORDING, OR OTHERWISE, WITHOUT THE PRIOR WRITTEN PERMISSION OF THE AUTHOR.

ANY VIOLATION BY STEALING THIS BOOK OR DOWNLOADING OR SHARING IT ILLEGALLY WILL BE PROSECUTED BY LAWYERS TO THE FULLEST EXTENT. THIS PUBLICATION IS PROTECTED UNDER THE US COPYRIGHT ACT OF 1976 AND ALL OTHER APPLICABLE INTERNATIONAL, FEDERAL, STATE AND LOCAL LAWS AND ALL RIGHTS ARE RESERVED, INCLUDING RESALE RIGHTS: YOU ARE NOT ALLOWED TO GIVE OR SELL THIS GUIDE TO ANYONE ELSE.

THIS PUBLICATION IS DESIGNED TO PROVIDE ACCURATE AND AUTHORITATIVE INFORMATION WITH REGARD TO THE SUBJECT MATTER COVERED. IT IS SOLD WITH THE UNDERSTANDING THAT THE AUTHORS AND PUBLISHERS ARE NOT ENGAGED IN RENDERING LEGAL, FINANCIAL, OR OTHER PROFESSIONAL ADVICE. LAWS AND PRACTICES OFTEN VARY FROM STATE TO STATE AND IF LEGAL OR OTHER EXPERT ASSISTANCE IS REQUIRED, THE SERVICES OF A PROFESSIONAL SHOULD BE SOUGHT. THE AUTHORS AND PUBLISHER SPECIFICALLY DISCLAIM ANY LIABILITY THAT IS INCURRED FROM THE USE OR APPLICATION OF THE CONTENTS OF THIS BOOK.

COPYRIGHT BY HOWEXPERT™ (OWNED BY HOT METHODS)
ALL RIGHTS RESERVED WORLDWIDE.

Table of Contents

Recommended Resources 2
Publisher's Foreword 3
Chapter 1: The Art and Love of Native American Beading 8
   Introduction: 8
   Beading Time is Sacred: 12
   Chapter Review: 15
Chapter 2: Beading Materials You May Want or Need 16
   Beads 16
   Threads 24
   Tools and Supplies 29
      Scissors: 29
      Needles: 29
      Pliers: 31
      Awls: 32
      A Glue Stick: 33
      A Lighter: 33
   Design and Patterns 34
   Miscellaneous Materials for Creating and Finishing .. 37
   Chapter Review: 39
Chapter 3: The Very Basics of Stringing Beads ... 41
   Stringing Beads 41
      Side note - Taking beads from a hank of beads: 43
      Stringing with simple beading thread: 45

Stringing multiple strands and using findings: 46
  Using Plastic-Coated Wire for stringing beads: 49
  Stringing with cord: 53
  Stringing beads with leather: 54
 Chapter Review: 63
Chapter 4: A Day for Daisy Chains 64
 Instructions: 64
  To begin: 65
  Here is your first lesson on hiding knots: 66
  Adding String to Your Project to Continue Beading: 72
 Chapter Review: 73
Chapter 5: The Brick Stitch 74
 Increasing Beads on a New Row of Brick Stitch 82
 Chapter Review: 89
Chapter 6: Mother Earth Medallion 90
 Chapter Review 104
Chapter 7: Going Crazy with the Peyote Stitch .105
 Adding and Subtracting Beads in Peyote Stitch: 115
 Tying in a new thread: 118
 If using a spoon handle instead of a feather: 121
 Chapter Review: 122
Chapter 8: Open Peyote Stitch 123
 Edge Stitch: 129
 Chapter Review: 145
Chapter 9: Loom Beading 146
 Chapter Review: 161

Chapter 10: Beaded Flat Work 162
  Chapter Review: *170*
Most Frequently Asked Questions About Native American Beading 171
About the Author 174
Recommended Resources 175

Chapter 1: The Art and Love of Native American Beading

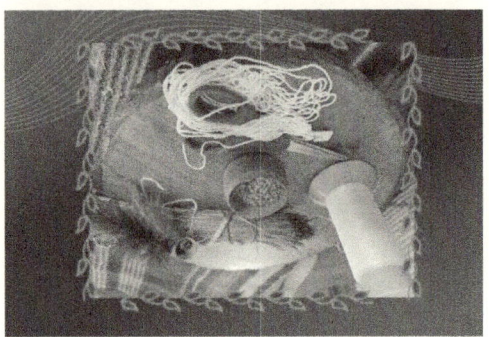

Introduction:

Hello, and welcome to your expert guide to Native American beading. I'm your expert guide, and I'm called **Little Blue Jay** in honor of my Native American Heritage. I've accumulated a lifetime of knowledge practicing this art with instruction in books and with other Native Americans. I was drawn to the art from the first time I ever saw beads. For me, to bead has always been to be at peace with God and the world around me.

My grandmother Vi was the one to teach me Native American beadwork at the age of six. She's not Native American but was very good at many crafts. And, she was raised on Native American reservations, so she learned the art from the source when she was a very young girl. Her father taught school during the hard years of the great depression, at times on reservations, and most of his students were from poor families. Vi's recounted stories of making doll clothes from animal skins as a child. Her beadwork through the years was exceptionally beautiful.

Curiously, my great-grandmother on my father's side was full-blooded Cherokee. Sadly, I never knew her, but her legacy is carried on through my beadwork and my children. Her name was Rhoda. We do not know her native name, as this was the case with many children from native tribes in her era. I know many people that had relatives of Native American descent who were incorporated into a different family without regard to the child's name or family history. But today, I choose to resurrect and honor their memory through my artwork with beads.

Tip #1 - *You don't have to be a Native American to learn this ancient art.*

It's available to everyone and a very popular form of artistic expression.

Native American beadwork has been in the process of development for over hundreds of years. The early American natives took pieces of bone they would carve into "Wampum." It was used for a monetary system and to show clan hierarchy.

Shells, porcupine quills, and various materials the natural world provided were all incorporated into the early art we call Native

American beadwork. Quills were cut and dyed and stitched to garments very early in their artwork. Glass beads replaced much of the use of quills because they were so much more durable and beautiful. However, many of the traditional patterns and symbols were then changed into the beadwork.

Many things in nature continue to be used as inspiration in this art form. Spirit animals such as bears, wolves, turtles, and eagles are just some of the iconic symbols many beaded pieces highlight. Native American tribes have stories passed down through the generations. These are also worked into designs they use that continue to tell their stories. Spider Woman, the trickster coyote, crows who were known to hunt with wolves in nature, and the coming of the White Buffalo are all interesting, legendary designs. Throughout the years, the creativity of Native Americans has been the ability to recognize beauty in nature and the culture of their heritage to express themselves.

Do you like detailed work that gives you unique jewelry and artwork? With Native American beadwork, you can create colorful and lovely pieces to enjoy for years. Yes, it's time-consuming, but you can also make small projects that can be completed easily. Every project I've ever attempted with beadwork has given me an outlet to expand my own creativity and diversify my sewing repertoire. I will provide you with some examples of similar crafts you may already be familiar with that will help you while learning to bead.

I liken the art of Native American *loom work* to cross-stitch. It also uses detailed, graphed designs, has a similar needle and thread experience, as well as counting out each row on the pattern as you go.

Flatwork pieces of beadwork are very much like embroidery. In flatwork beading, you use an embroidery hoop as needed, and your beads are sewn onto the fabric of your choice. There are no fancy knots or stitches with Native American flatwork, but there is a method of laying down the beads for best results. And you can add embroidery along with the beaded design as you like. There are no hard fast rules in Native American beading. It is constantly evolving.

And then, we come to the *Daisy Chain, Peyote, Open Peyote,* and *Brick Stitch*, the like of which is closest to weaving or macrame. Only with these stitches, there is one simple stitch you repeat over and over to gain the weave effect.

As you can see, having any knowledge of sewing techniques will already stand you in good stead, but it's not necessary. We will begin with simple ways of stringing and weaving beads and progress to the more complicated stitches.

I'm positive the very first instructions will give you projects that can be crafted and enjoyed by you alone. Read through and scan all the chapters on the different stitches. You don't have to start with the first one. I've simply listed the least complex to the most time inclusive. Go as you feel comfortable.

And the very best thing about Native American beadwork is—beads! So if you love beads and shiny things, then this is a great craft choice.

My mother always told me she thought I was born part crow because of how I loved shiny beads. They are my treasure. And this craft is a gift I give from one crow to another. It can bless you, your family, and your friends and carry a long tradition of beauty forward to another generation.

How wonderful is that? Yes, and you can be a part of this. Be patient with yourself, with your thread, and remember to take a breath through the hard parts, and don't give up. Every path in the forest is littered with obstacles for your moccasins to step around. That is all. And I will lead you through this forest, giving you expert tips and advice along the way to take you through to a brilliant finish. You will look back at the forest from the top of a mountain view, wondering why you thought it was so difficult.

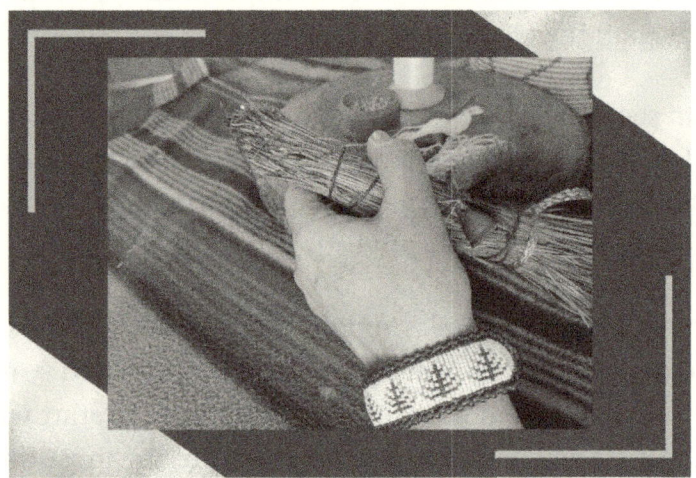

Beading Time is Sacred:

Tip #2 - Set your beading time apart in special ways that make it sacred for you.

It will be more satisfying, help you concentrate, and not let distractions interfere.

My beading time becomes more sacred to me as the years go by. I had the privilege to bead with groups of women in Washington state years ago. These fellow Native Americans possessed traditions handed down through their families. Sometimes we began our beading by setting this time apart as special with "smudging." Usually, a smudge stick is made of sage or other naturally good-smelling materials. Smudging is meant to clear the air from negativity and help you focus on a productive and bonding time together.

I show a smudge stick in the above picture made from pine needles. As you can see, it's simply a bundle of dried pine needles wrapped with string or leather. I trim the top and bottom, so it's not messy looking. The sage sticks are similarly made. Some people use smudging to clear the air of negativity. I don't believe there's magic in these, but the magic is what you do within your heart and mind. It's a simple focusing technique for me.

And celebrating life and art also begins with appreciation. What we appreciate, we treat differently. Time spent with friends and family, creativity being explored through your crafting or the simplicity of quiet contemplation, and being still in such a busy world is found to become more important as the river of life takes us along within its banks. We *learn* appreciation. Setting this time apart in special ways is one way to learn the art of appreciation and celebration.

Tip #3 - *Beadwork is very easy to take while you travel verses other crafts.*

With beading supplies, the components are usually small, and the pieces and tools are minimal, making beadwork very easy to pack along to a doctor appointment, car ride, or other times we simply have to *wait* in life. It redeems time in a productive way.

I find beadwork to be very soothing, and the act of beading keeps my mind supple and helps prevent aging. If that isn't something to celebrate, I don't know what is!

Anyway, whatever ways you would like to honor this time in your own life, I think it will help you progress and succeed. And you will find yourself "seeing" nature and the world around you quite differently. You will discover treasures in this world you weren't expecting.

I hope you enjoy the chapters to come. But don't be discouraged if this compilation seems overwhelming. I know you can succeed! Remember, I began at the age of six. I challenged myself my whole life to add to my knowledge of Native American beadwork, and there are countless hours of experience included. You, however, have a book with expert advice to help you from point A to B much faster than I managed.

When I began, there wasn't much written on the subject of Native American beadwork. I am very excited now when seeing the beautiful loom work patterns offered online and the various books and materials easily bought from bead stores around the country.

And make no mistake, beading is very time-consuming. Typically, I find it takes about an hour a square inch. But it is time well spent. Take one stitch at a time and get familiar with them all. Some will not be as appealing, while some you may find absorb your attention. You will begin to see and find ways to incorporate them together for fantastic projects only you could create. That's when you know you have become an expert beader as well.

Tip #4 - When your thread gets hung up or tangled, relax and gently pull the knot or tangle outward to begin unraveling.

The thread is problematic as it's so thin, but opening the knots and tangles gives you the opportunity to unravel your problematic thread and continue beading. Otherwise, and if it's simply impossible to unravel, you will need to cut the thread and tie a knot at the beadwork, carefully burn the ends, re-thread your needle, and continue as if adding thread.

As with anything in life, time and practice will reduce the stress of it.

Have faith in yourself, and have fun!

Chapter Review:

- You can use things around you to incorporate into your beading.
- Your beadwork can be a way to honor the history of Native Americans.
- You can make your beading time special and sacred.
- Advice and encouragement are given by your expert beader.

Chapter 2: Beading Materials You May Want or Need

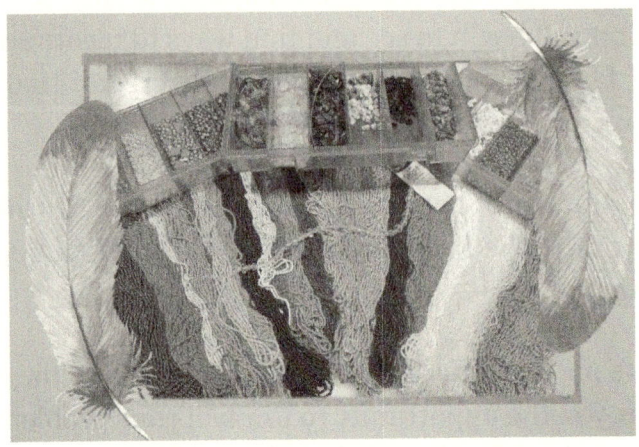

Beads

There are a LOT of different beads in the world. The beads we are interested in for the basic Native American beading are seed beads. But seed beads as we know them didn't really come around until after other countries began exploring and mapping North America.

The original beads were made of pieces of bone and tusks, and antlers and used for money. Native Americans traded them as money called *Wampum*. They would break and sand the hard pieces to the wanted length, laboriously bore into them from one end and then the other end. It's one-way archaeologists can verify the age of bone-type beads. The earlier beads show an uneven hole through them from the rudimentary tools of the period.

Native Americans also used porcupine quills in their adornments and other natural things such as shells and seeds. *This is perhaps why we call the smaller beads today seed beads.*

Many Native American tribes used beads for money and adornment. Basically, the earliest glass beads came to them from Venice. Other beads, called Trade Beads, or Millefiori beads, were also brought from Venice around the early 1800s. They are very colorful and larger than we will be using in our book.

Holland also sold beads to traders going to the Americas, and Czechoslovakia eventually became the dominant supplier later on. The Hudson Bay Trading Company, a compilation of adventurous explorers, brought many beads in the early 1900s to North America. They were intent on trade in the new country, and Native Americans were eager to trade for beads.

Tip #5 - *Seed beads are tiny and vary in size on a scale that goes up in number value as the size of the bead gets smaller.*

So, the bigger the size number, the smaller the bead. The holes in a bead seem to vary in size more so than the circumference of the outside area.

Beads and needles are sized together just like wire in your hardware store. Bead sizes can gauge at many levels, but for our usual beading purposes, they begin about size 8, up to a tiny, tiny bead, size 18. I have done very few projects with size 18 beads, and these are usually found in antique stores on small hanks with a string that is brown from age. You may find sizes 16-18 online, but they are not common to come across.

I've never come across any smaller beads than size 18, and I highly recommend you don't use anything larger than size 10 for our purposes. The only exception to using the larger beads would be to incorporate them into the stringing of a necklace or as a clasp-type use.

I also advise you to buy all the same-sized beads for the main body of your work. Edgings can be somewhat larger, but only by one size for best results. So if you weave a bracelet with size 11 beads, then a size 10 bead would be appropriate to finish an edging. You can also use the same-sized beads for edgings, just like your main body of work. I will go over this again in our section on edging, so you don't have to remember until we get there.

Size 10 beads are often used to teach children or beginners uncomfortable with smaller beads. You may also see these larger beads used in machine-produced beadwork.

Tip #6 - *If you use a larger-sized bead, you will lose some of your ability to build a pattern that's very intricate.*

Unless you want a HUGE piece of beadwork without much detail, then use the smaller-sized beads.

The more strings your pattern will require, the wider your work gets, especially if you use larger seed beads. For example, I usually work in size 12 beads. But size 11 beads are a tad larger and easier to move your needle and thread through.

Tip #7 - *Use size 11 beads to begin learning Native American bead stitches.*

They are usually large enough to pass your needle through easily and will give you added creativity in making patterns.

After traders came to North America, seed beads were a hit among natives. They bought everything from directions in the new world, needed supplies, to land. Original beads used in early beadwork came from several sources mentioned already.

African trade beads are often seen among original Native American work. They actually come from Venice, not Africa. Many trade beads, just like the original ones traded with Native Americans, can still be found. You will recognize them as the hanks are usually stranded on sinew or leather. They are larger, brightly colored, or look like the red earth itself in Africa. While these are very colorful and beautiful, they usually aren't small enough for our beading needs.

Most all seed beads made of glass were made in Venice and Czechoslovakia. These have been the primary producers of glass seed beads in an astonishing array of colors and styles. Czechoslovakia is still a leading manufacturer of glass beads today, but other countries are coming into the market with beautiful versions of the same.

If you find a certain supplier of beads you like, then try to find your colors for your work among one supplier. This ensures a more uniform pattern at the end of your hours of work. The manufacturing process differs among the suppliers, which causes slight differences. Each manufacturer can be distinct in the size of the bead and the hole of the bead, even if it's measured with the same parameters.

And even among glass seed beads, there are a lot of differences. There are specialty ones that come in little tubes made expressly with larger holes for needles to pass. They can also be more uniform. Seed beads, in general, are more oblong than wide. Look closely at what you're ordering or buying to see if they are uniform and that the holes are somewhat open for easier sewing.

Price is important, and beading isn't necessarily a cheap hobby, but you want to choose, remembering that you will spend hours on a single piece of work, and it's worth more to invest smartly into the beads than not.

Tip #8 - Use the same gauged needle as the size of the bead you are stringing.

With some exceptions, this allows you to accomplish multiple passes inside the hole of a bead along with the thread.

Tip #9 - I highly recommend you don't use plastic beads.

Your time into a crafted piece will be rewarded with glass beads as they maintain their shine and sparkle long after plastic ones will dull and lose the cut edges that catch the light.

Among glass seed beads you will find some main categories:

- A solid color with no particular glisten and solid beads that are a "flat" color. Similar to buying paint with no gloss
- Solid colored beads with a pearl-like gloss, or solid with an iridescent glaze finish.
- Solid color metallic-finished beads. These are highly suspect! Be warned. Except for the more expensive ones, many of these lose their metallic finish, so don't invest them into a piece you hope to own for years to come. They are really wonderful for a pair of earrings or other pieces you may not expect to keep for a long time.
- There are clear glass beads with colored centers. The color shines from within, but they will appear somewhat see-through in the light.
- Colored glass beads with a silver-lined hole. These have extra shine from the silver lining beneath the colored glass. A beautiful choice to add extra shine to your work.

- Tri-cut and bi-cut glass beads sparkle the best, stay beautiful for years to come, and "pop" in your beadwork. The only drawback to these is they are really good at cutting your thread.
- Bugle beads are a longer version of the seed bead. They are gauged the same and look like a long tube of glass. Some are only a bit longer than regular seed beads, while others can be as long as an inch or an inch and a half. I find these beads very usable when adding dangles to a piece. They have very sharp edges and will strip or cut your thread, so beware. I very rarely use them, but many people do wonderful work with them.
- And lastly, the main seed bead categories should include the ancient *white-heart* bead. The colored glass has a white coating in the center around the hole of the bead so that the colored glass glows like a solid color from within, something like a silver-lined bead. They last better than the silver-lined beads, in my experience. If you're lucky enough to find smaller-sized white hearts, buy them!

Tip #10 - Don't use tri-cut or bi-cut beads in beadwork pieces that move a lot, like dangles on earrings.

The edges of these beads are sharp, and the movement over time cuts the threads of the beadwork. Therefore, you will do better to use them in flatwork or within the woven part of brick stitch, peyote, open peyote, and even in loom work where they are supported by other beads around them and less likely to experience a lot of movement.

Tip #11 - Use beeswax on your beading thread when using bugle, tri-cut, or bi-cut beads.

It protects the thread from these sharper-edged beads.

So what about all the other beads? Well, yes, there are a LOT of other beads to choose from for a lot of different uses. I can't possibly cover them all here. They are also varied and beautiful.

When you get more familiar with the individual stitches, you can weave larger beads over the top of a piece, use them in the stringing of the necklace part that attaches to something like a medicine pouch or even add them at the top of an earring, and incorporate them into dangles at uniform places.

These larger beads are all used in the finishing part of this particular kind of work.

Tip #12 - *If you want the metallic look for your beadwork, use the more expensive silver or gold-plated beads.*

The coatings don't flake off like cheaper metallic bead varieties.

So, let's include some info about these larger types of decorative beads:

- Bone beads can be interesting and usually come in a barrel shape or long bead. They are carved into skulls and cut to make patterns along the bead. Some long spiral ones are very nice, and bone beads make especially nice *spacer* beads. Spacer beads are used when adding multiple strands to a piece, like a bracelet or necklace. They have multiple holes to space the strands at a regulated distance. Mostly, spacer beads are used for stringing necklaces or bracelets and not for our woven beadwork.
- I have always admired lampwork beads. You will usually find them to be more than one color of glass. They are an art all by themselves. They tend to run larger but can come in all kinds of shapes. I once saw a stupendous necklace at the

market in Seattle made of lampwork *teapot-shaped* beads. Many lampwork beads are hand-blown, and most will have nothing to do with our work here except to add to a piece already crafted with seed beads.

- Semi-precious stone beads are an excellent choice for Native American beadwork. Predominantly, you will see turquoise used the most in a variety of ways in Native American beadwork.
- If you see hanks of semi-precious stone beads, they are usually in the form of chips. Chips are irregular pieces polished and strung on a single hank when buying. The other kind of semi-precious stone beads are either round or shaped like a tube, and some may even look like animals or stars, and so on. Stone, semi-precious beads, are polished and graded in size as well. I highly recommend using them for your work where you can.

Tip #13 – *Semi-precious stone beads will cost a bit more because the process of cutting the stone lends itself to cracking.*

The chips or other shaped beads are the result of the stone pieces that withstood the cutting and polishing ordeal and didn't break.

And then, there are the favorite crystal beads which are also graded into gauged sizes. They come in all colors, are fantastically beautiful, and catch the light. They make strands of these in smaller sizes too. I mostly use them to accentuate beadwork, but I've seen Native American regalia that has loads of sparkle from tri-cuts and crystals. Crystals are usually found on a single hank and will cost you more. But they're worth it. And I haven't noticed them cutting my thread like the tri-cuts or bi-cut seed beads.

Tip #14 - Buy white and black seed beads as a staple for your work.

White "pops" any color it's against in a pattern, and lends a very clean and bright effect. Black is helpful as an outline, border, or solid background.

Tip #15 - Be careful when buying beads.

It's very addictive!

Threads

I use all kinds of threads like the ones above. But for Native American beadwork, you need *beading* thread. Unfortunately, it can NOT usually be found in your local craft stores, even though they label some thread as such, but it will only be available online or found at an actual bead store. I have seen it offered in craft stores, but I've rarely found any that comes near the strength and slickness of the real stuff. Slick is important as well. Straight cotton thread is problematic for that reason.

Tip #16 - To tell the difference in beading threads to find the "good" stuff, I pull off about a foot of it and try to break it.

Proper thread for beadwork almost slices into my fingers if it's the good stuff before it will break. But it's difficult to do that if you don't want to buy it first. I invest a bit extra into a spool of the good stuff when I find it in a real bead store or an online beading supply site. I've found a larger spool lasts for years.

If you look in a craft store in the sewing department, you can find spools of embroidery floss in white and other colors that can work just as well. You'll need a single strand-type embroidery floss that comes on a spool, as the usual embroidery thread has multiple strands. That doesn't work at all! It's too wide to go through the eye of our tiny needles, and most of our work will pass through the hole of a bead at least twice or more. Thread is gauged as well, so look for the smallest gauge you can find.

Avoid any thread purely made of cotton. Cotton thread likes to twist and knot as you work, even if using beeswax before you begin. I do use heavy cotton thread for stringing the strands of a necklace at times because using bead thread can be prone to breaking under the pull of the main beadwork that is hanging from it. It's also OK to use a heavier cotton thread in the outside threads of a loom piece. But the heavier thread will show in your finished piece. Again, it's used for strength and in places where you aren't weaving anything with it.

Native Americans use sinew thread a lot in other kinds of work, but sometimes it's used in beadwork. You can strand beads with it for necklaces, and the sinew can be pulled apart for smaller threads if you want to. Cut it to the length you need, pull one end of it open so that you see the individual strands, and gently pull them apart, going down the length of the sinew.

Here is an image of sinew with the end being unraveled. This also works with embroidery thread if you want to go to the trouble of separating the strands for use in beadwork.

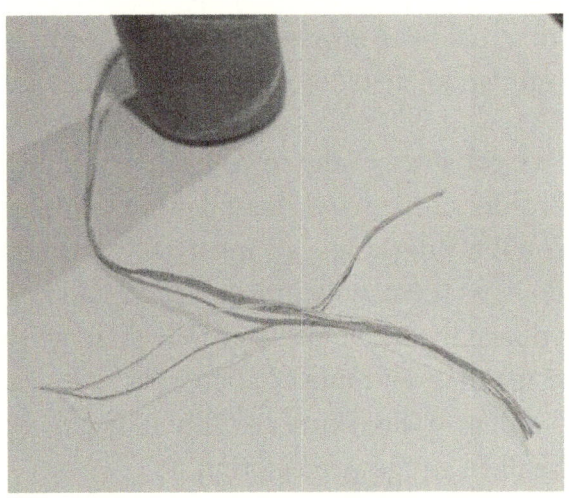

Mostly you will see beading thread offered in white and black.

Tip #17 - Black thread sometimes is brittle and will break, so test it before beginning.

I don't know why black thread is prone to do this; that's simply your tip from my experience with it!

Most beading thread begins at size 00. It goes up from there. Unless you are beading very tiny-sized beads, size 00 is not strong enough for most beadwork. Try something thicker than that.

I also use the coated wire that is found for making jewelry. When I want a single strand of beads that will be very strong, I use the coated wire. It's small enough to string using size 8-10 beads. With a strong strand of beads, you can attach your beadwork or add more of the same beaded strands as you like without worrying about breakage.

However, don't use this coated wire for tight necklaces you can't slip over your head, or bracelets, because it doesn't break if caught in something that could harm you. Never wear these if working around machinery. It could pull you into the machine or be pulled so hard to slice into you. This stuff is very strong. It's unlikely but possible.

And then, when using beading string, many Native Americans run a chunk of beeswax over it before beading. I have a small piece as an example in the picture above. Beeswax does help protect your thread from the elements it may encounter over time. I especially like to use it for the main strings on my loom before I begin the beadwork itself.

Tip #18 - Press your beeswax into the strings and gently slide across them, or pull the string along against the beeswax to properly coat your strings.

Beeswax can "gum up" a bit. It's OK, just rub a soft piece of leather over them and smooth the beeswax if that happens. The warmer the beeswax gets from the friction, the softer it becomes and smooths out. Just be patient and gentle with your thread.

I've found that beeswax can hinder your dangles from moving with as much freedom, so try it and see what you think. Here again, long-term projects I want to preserve for years would benefit from beeswax, but it's not necessary.

Lastly, There's sinew. It was originally made of animals killed for survival. The Native Americans used all the animals possible. This string is also a factor in authenticating Native American beadwork or garments. Before they had any kind of cotton thread, they used sinew. It's usually a brown-colored thread. It looks like it's waxy and can vary in color from very light tans to darker browns. You can find sinew in craft stores, but don't expect it to be authentic. It is especially strong if used for stringing necklaces or sewing articles of clothing and purses or bags. Unlike leather strands, sinew is more like string.

Tip #19 - Whatever thread you buy for your project, give it the TEST.

Take a piece about a foot long and try to break it with your hands. If it's going to work for beading, it shouldn't break easily. And twist it and see if it tries to knot up.

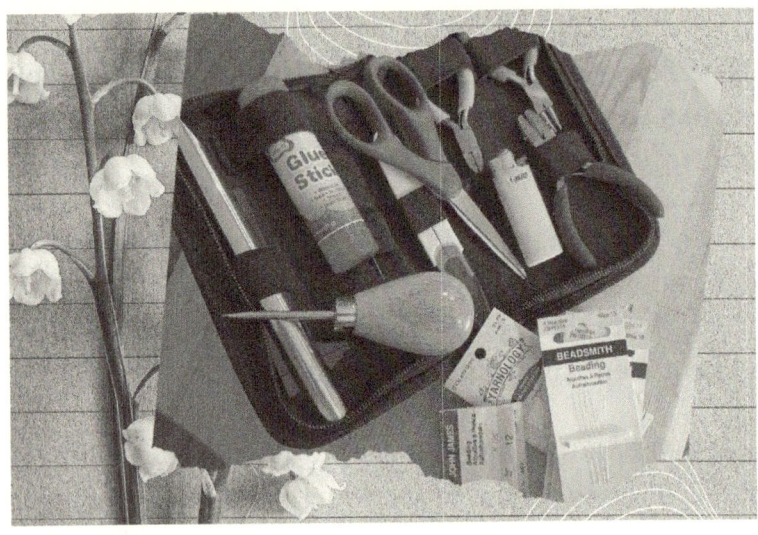

Tools and Supplies

- The basic tools you will need:
- Good scissors with a sharp edge to the end
- Needles gauged to the same size as your beads
- Side-cutting pliers to cut coated wire if you are using it.
- Regular small needle-nosed pliers
- An awl you can use to ream beads
- A regular glue stick for crafts
- A lighter

Scissors:

Smaller scissors just work better with beadwork. You can use larger ones, but the point will be too wide to get into the small spaces required in beadwork. I've never had to buy any specialty brand or kind, and you can find them just about anywhere sewing stuff is offered. Buy the kind that isn't rounded at the end but pointed and sharp to the tip.

Needles:

Needles are a real adventure to find at times. The basic sized 10, 11, 12, and 13 can mostly be had in craft stores and beading stores. Size 14, 15, 16, or 18 have incredibly small eyes when threading and aren't as readily available. I don't usually see sizes 13 or 14. It tends to skip to below and above. And size 18 is practically non-existent. Size 15 works for most of the small beads, but you will be limited to passing through them only once, or perhaps twice.

Tip #20 - Use the same sized needle as the beads in your work when possible.

You can always use a smaller needle with bigger beads, but not the other way around.

Depending on the work you're doing, how many times the needle will have to pass through the bead, and if you're using single or double strands, then using one sized larger needle could work in a smaller bead. But mostly, plan on using the same size bead as the needle. This is because they are conveniently gauged for each other.

If you're sewing onto leather for a flat piece of work or attaching beadwork to leather, then leather needles will be needed. Leather needles are gauged the same as any other kind. They are different in that they have a pointed end with two or three cuts to make them slide through the hide easier. You can look at the end of the needle and see the angles cut away from the metal tip.

Tip #21 - Be very careful when using leather needles.

They are made to go through leather, so your finger is no obstacle.

Here is where using your needle-nosed pliers comes in handy to grip and pull the needle through the leather instead of using your fingers.

I've found it difficult to purchase these needles in sizes smaller than size 10. But *Glover* brand does make them in smaller gauges. I've only come across odd packages of them in little corner trading companies and online.

As for regular needles, any needle smaller than size 13 may give you trouble. They are difficult to thread. I have no advice to offer except to get a magnifying glass and consider the necessity of such a small bead choice. It will be a challenge, and I suggest you only use a single strand to bead with, no doubling of your thread for strength. Even with a small needle, the tiny beads can only be passed through maybe twice. Three times is not the charm in beadwork, unlike the old saying otherwise.

Pliers:

Side-cutting pliers are definitely used for anything with wire or coated wire that may be a part of your project. However, you may not need these to start with unless you are using wire.

Needle-nose pliers are almost a must. I prefer them flat inside, not rounded tips like wire-wrapping pliers. It's also helpful if they have ridged teeth inside. I use them to grab my needle in a tight spot and pull the bead through whatever is causing resistance. Sometimes the bead breaks, but it mostly comes out OK if you go slowly and pull steady.

I also use these pliers to break a bead as my project progresses when there are more beads than necessary. That way, I don't have to un-thread the work, which is a lot more trouble. This is usually a problem when beginning a peyote piece. Unless I've done the piece already, the beginning strand of beads is guesswork, and breaking out beads is necessary.

Some beaders use rounded needle-nosed pliers, but that's mostly for metal wire work or jewelry findings. You can use round-nose or needle-nose pliers to work with any findings we may discuss. Rounded needle-nosed pliers are smooth and less likely to scar the metal pieces; this is why they are used for wire wrapping.

Tip #22 - Findings are the metal pieces used in making jewelry.

Examples include necklace clasps, earring hoops, or copper bands for inside bracelets. There are thousands of jewelry findings you can use in Native American beadwork when finishing and constructing your piece.

Awls:

The awl is a traditional Native American tool. Young girls sewed a pouch as one of their first projects and adorned it with beadwork or other things to hold the basic tools they would need to survive. An awl was one of the tools traditionally held in the pouch. It resembles an ice pick. It's used a lot in leatherwork as well and is good for piercing holes through the leather so straps can be threaded through and make clothes or pouches, and so forth.

We use it for the larger beads we may want to thread onto sinew or leather strands. It's inserted into a bead to twist inside and make the hole of the bead larger. This works for a lot of beads, but ones made of glass can break if you don't go slowly. A special awl is used for beads. It's been roughened for this purpose. Regular smooth awls won't be as effective.

The only time you may want to use an awl is if your finishing beads need to be adjusted to be threaded through with leather or sinew. Or, if your beadwork is being sewn onto leather and you need to pierce a hole in the leather.

A Glue Stick:

Yep, a plain old glue stick will serve you well in beading. It's simple and effective on many types of materials. I've almost given up on specialty glues altogether. Glue sticks will adhere the leather together, pieces of cloth, or other materials you may use in your beading. It's the easiest, least messy way of gluing anything. Glue sticks are predominately used only in the finishing of your work.

A Lighter:

It seems weird, right? What could a lighter have to do with beadwork? Well, just as the Native Americans I regularly sat with in beading circles, who would use beeswax for their thread, we would also use a lighter to burn the ends of a knot. It's that simple but very important. Burning the ends of your knots keeps them from unraveling and gets rid of extra thread that may not have been cut so close.

Be very careful when burning your cut threads in tight places; you can burn through important threads holding your work together.

A lighter can also be used in the finishing of your work to keep the edge of some materials from fraying. Leather is, by far, one of the best materials to use if you can, as it doesn't fray.

Tip #23 - Your best tool for beading success is ... Patience!

Being in a hurry will cause mistakes, and you will not enjoy the experience as much.

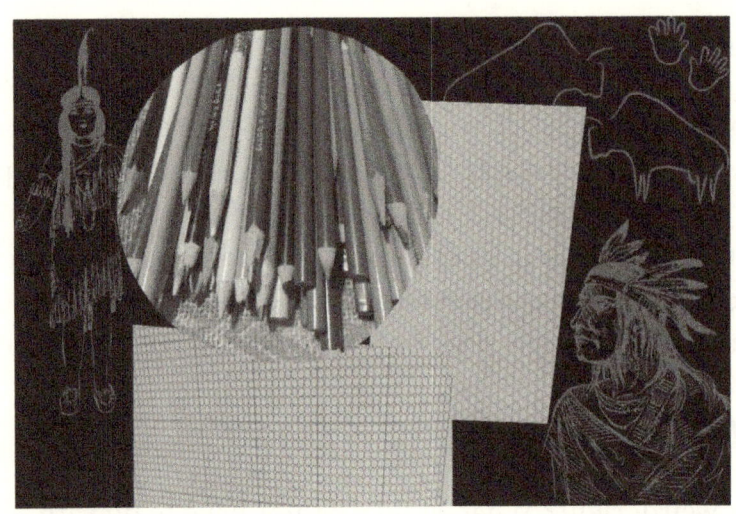

Design and Patterns

I could write a whole book just on this subject alone. However, the traditional patterns of many Native American tribes are well documented and available if you have a certain tribe in mind. The patterns of the Native Americans, here again, reflect the world around them, the Great Spirit who created it all, and daily life within their tribes.

The picture of an arrow is used a lot in designs, as well as thunderheads and wolves or coyotes. Eagles are a phenomenal centerpiece, and I've seen intricate work done with those. Flowers are usually seen in patterns on female *regalia*. And the pattern called "fire colors" is often used across the different tribes. As you can imagine, the bead colors sit beside each other, from white or yellows to oranges and reds, and even greens, or blue and turquoise, and they are used together for very bright effects like flames of fire. I have a project coming up for you in this book using fire colors. Bright, and fun!

I've used felt-tipped markers to create patterns in the past, but I've found the colored pencils to be better. They usually offer a better range of colors and can be erased if needed as you create your pattern. Felt pens are definitely brighter for patterns, but if I have to change a boo-boo in a pattern, you can't erase them. And yes, experts make boo-boos all the time!

There are several ways to make a pattern for beadwork. You can draw your own beads in a row and color them, use regular graph paper you can find almost anywhere, or order special bead graph paper online. I started making my own by hand, but I do advise using the online beading graph paper if you can afford it. You can buy some really cheaply and photocopy them as you need. Basically, whatever you choose, you simply color in the dots to create whatever pattern you like. I would look online for ideas and patterns related to the Native American tribe you may want to emulate. There are loads of patterns now for sale, but you can get inspiration just by looking.

Three types of patterns are used for Native American beadwork.

One has beads stacked directly on top of one another and is used for loom work.

Another kind has beads that are shown interlocking one another like bricks in a wall. This one is used for Peyote stitches where the beads are turned with their length going up and down. Remember, beads are oblong, and the patterns reflect that.

If you turn the peyote type of paper sideways, the beads are still interlocking, but the pattern looks like bricks stacked in a wall. This is used for brick stitch; called that for this very reason.

With these two types of pattern paper, you should be able to work out a pattern you like for most projects. I am not going to include examples of patterns here, just the materials, but you will understand all of this better as you progress to the chapters on the individual stitches. You will see my photos of beadwork. I've done. You are welcome to copy these patterns as you like.

Flatwork is the other type of pattern you will make. A flatwork pattern is a sketch or stencil of anything you like. It's more of a free-hand type drawing but can be an overlay pattern you can find in embroidery or other crafts you may acquire anywhere. It's up to you what you want to bead. This pattern will simply be transferred onto a piece of material for flatwork. As you do more projects, you'll have an easier time deciding.

Making patterns is one of the most creative parts of Native American beading. **The colors, the shapes, and the spirit of your design will be birthed here.** This is where you can distinguish your art from anyone else. I will begin incorporating pattern skills for you to use as we go through each section, so don't worry; you will have a lot of opportunities to learn this as we go deeper into our instructions.

Remember, even a simple pattern for beadwork makes an object you decorate special. It shows you have a work ethic that not only includes the normal effort but separates everyday objects into something extravagant and a joy to wear or use. I've seen purses, jackets, aprons, flashlights, pipes, lighters, and many other beaded items that made them stand out.

Expert Tip #24 - Make sure you have a really good eraser when designing your patterns.

Mistakes happen, even to experts.

Miscellaneous Materials for Creating and Finishing

After you make your pattern, pick out your beads, weave them together; then, what do you need? Well, for starters, it depends on what you're making. You will, at the very least, most likely need *findings*. These are the things jewelers use to finish a piece of jewelry. They are the earring hangers, hooks, clasps, spacers, and usually metal things for making your beadwork usable. I have also seen some very nice spacers made of bone.

Example: I use copper bands quite often that are bendable for bracelets. They are a very plain band of copper and work as a form to mount my beadwork upon. First, I cover them with some type of material or leather, using my glue stick to adhere the material to the copper band before sewing the edges together. Then,

I mount the beadwork by sewing it onto the material on the copper band and finish my bracelet with an edging stitch to hide any imperfections and knots from sewing.

Tip #25 - Findings will be just as much a part of many of your projects as the beadwork itself.

They also will be a *part of the design*, especially with necklaces and earrings.

(I will cover more about this as we go further into different stitches and finishing your projects.)

So, the basics for finishing beadwork are certain materials such as leather or whatnot, strong thread, a glue stick, and various findings. If you're making a purse, then you need a plain purse to adorn, and so on. You get the idea. I have used pieces of antique jewelry and interesting buttons for finishing pieces of work, all the way to beading around cabochons or coins.

Tip #26 - Look around you for items to use in your own beadwork.

This is exactly what authentic Native Americans used and still do. You will see many with curled snuff can lids used for "bells" along the bottom of skirts. Traditions start with an idea that is carried along through the next generation. Use what is available to you. It may start a new tradition.

I often use a cool wobbly looking stick to hang beadwork from. You can even bead around the stick to continue the theme. Basically, almost anything can be incorporated into Native American beadwork. For example, I saw a beautiful work of Peyote stitching done around a simple cattail. For someone to bead around what others most often think of as a common weed in the ditch is just perfect for some artists.

You could possibly use a hot glue gun for your work, but I would be careful. The glue tends to harden and cause lumps beneath beadwork. In addition, I find hot glue to be very limited as it's prone to separate with temperature changes.

Tip #27 - Remember when gluing anything, it's best to use an edge stitch and sew it together as well.

Whatever is glued when finishing your work will be more secure if it's stitched as well to help it hold together over time.

Tip #28 - Finishing your beadwork. can be tedious.

It can take as much time, patience, and thought as the beadwork itself.

Chapter Review:

- We learned about the different sizes and kinds of beads and what they are used for.
- We were given some facts about the history of the origin of beads in Native American beadwork.
- We learned about different types of beading threads and how to use them.
- Needle types and gauges were explained, and how to select the particular needles we will need.
- We learned about the different kinds of pliers and how to use them.

- We explored some facts about the history and uses of the awl.
- We were given examples of three pattern papers we can use for certain stitches.
- Information about using jewelry findings was explored and explained.
- We were encouraged to incorporate objects around us into our finishing work that could be unusual or distinguish originality.

Chapter 3: The Very Basics of Stringing Beads

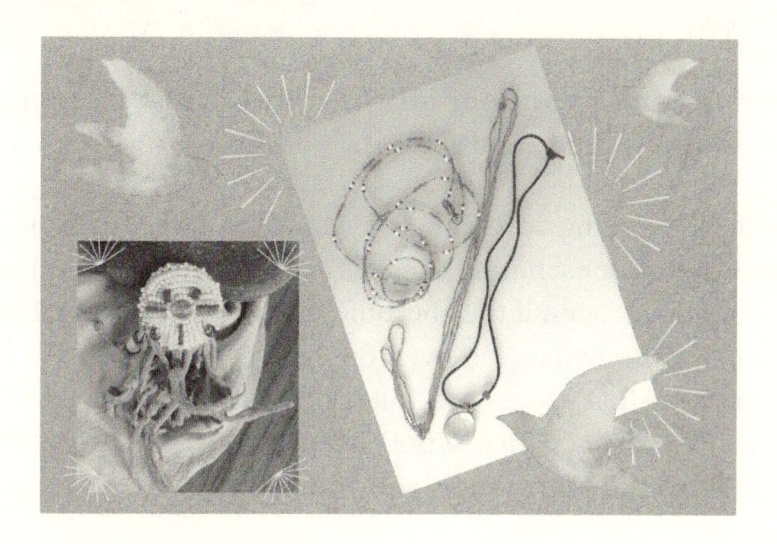

Stringing Beads

This may seem rather basic for some of our readers, but we have to start here. And stringing beads is a lot of fun. Some people see hanks of beads in bead stores and think they are strung already. But that is how many beads have been bought and sold for decades. Stringing beads is very important in that it will get you familiar with holding your needle and thread and making knots if you're new at this. I usually make square knots which is a simple loop, and you go back through the loop once or twice to make a knot.

You will find your own ways of making knots, holding the beadwork and thread as you go, and unraveling unwanted knots that "happen" along the way. Learning how to physically hold and pull the thread through your beadwork will also teach you how to avoid your thread knotting up as much.

You will enjoy the process. And don't worry about time lost having to figure this stuff out. Every bit of this is teaching you to handle your needle and thread better, which is really important in the later stitches.

Tip #29 - Using a random mix of colors with stringing beads creates a beautiful effect.

As you begin creating different projects, you will see that you have a few beads left over each time. It takes an impossible amount of time to separate them again if they become mixed, or there aren't enough for another project when left over. So, I always end up with a bowl of mixed beads that are just for fun projects like stringing necklaces and bracelets. Mixed with a variety of specialty beads as you string them, you can still utilize your leftover beads.

Side note - Taking beads from a hank of beads:

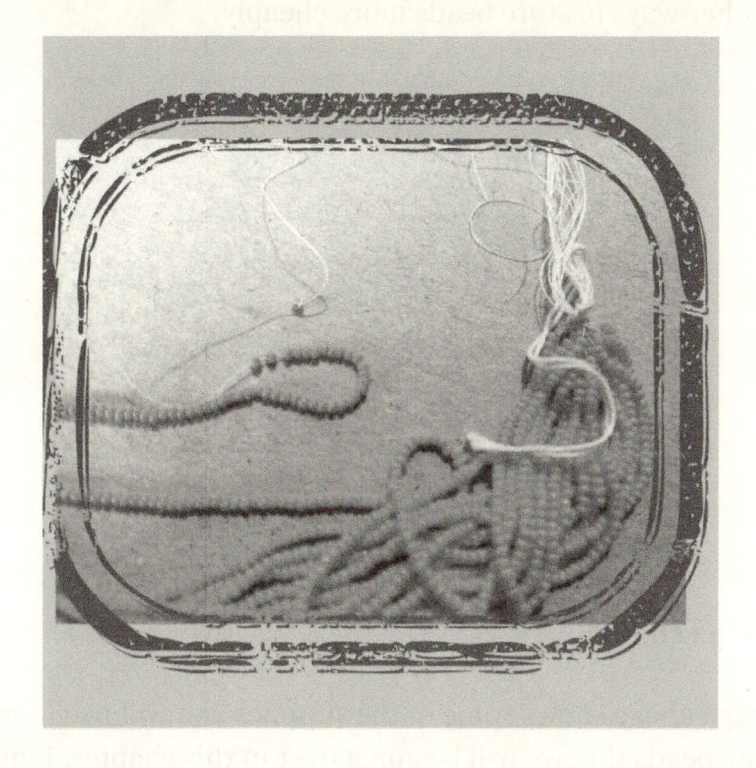

It can be frustrating to simply need five beads of a certain color from a hank of beads. This simple trick will keep you from ending up with a lot of scattered beads. Simply pull or cut one strand away from the hank at one end of the strand. Slide off how many beads you need, then tie the bottom bead onto the hank thread as shown above.

Tip #30 - Store your hanks of seed beads in plastic freezer bags.

I've tried multiple containers for tiny seed beads. But either you can't see through them, or they don't contain the small beads well, or, egad, the tops of tubes fall off constantly. I've found simple baggies work very well and store easily. I invest just a bit more into the freezer bags for durability. I guarantee you there are few, if none, other ways to store beads more cheaply.

So, let's get started!

The image above shows some of the supplies you will need for stringing beads that we will be going over in this chapter. I included my bowl of leftover beads, and this is only a small part of the beads you will have left over in time. I picked out some larger beads as well as semi-precious birds to add to the mix-up for the necklace we will make. Metal findings are shown above, along with the circular plastic holder shown. This is how the coated wire is sold. You can see the small silver metal crimping beads you will use with the plastic-coated wire. These crimping beads come in other colored metals as well.

I will lead you through a few basic projects, beginning with basic stringing with thread, then using the wire, and finally, using sinew or leather for a beadwork project.

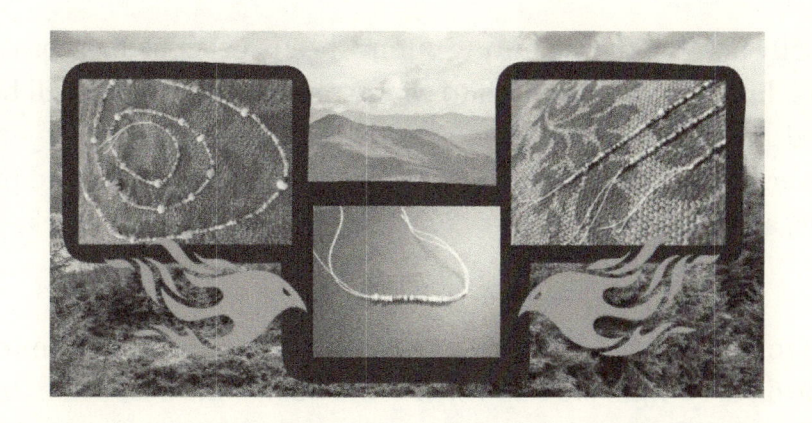

Stringing with simple beading thread:

We will begin by pulling out enough thread to slip easily over your head as a necklace.

Tip #31 - Double your thread in projects where possible.

Especially if a lot of weight will be held by the strand.

Double the amount of thread so that it's twice as much as you need. Include enough thread to leave at least a 2- to 3-inch tail on both ends.

Thread on your needle to accommodate the smallest sized beads you will be using for your project. Threading beading needles can be a chore. It takes time and practice, and sometimes someone with better eyes to help you where needed.

Tie both ends together now, leaving a 2- to 3-inch tail behind the knot, as shown above in the middle picture. Next, begin threading on your beads just as in the same middle picture, and continue until you have the whole necklace strung with your beads.

I usually don't bother counting out my beads when using mixed colors, but I do pay attention to where my specialty beads will be placed. In my necklace above, I've used a combination of my leftover beads, some #8 turquoise *white hearts*, #8 white and pink beads, and I've included a few *lapis lazuli,* semi-precious rock, birds.

I had to think about which way to thread the birds on as I wanted my birds to be right side up when I finished. Some beads like this are directional. Just imagine the necklace draping as when you will be wearing it, and you'll see which way to thread them on.

In the top left picture, you can see my finished strand. I always recommend you use a double strand of thread for this type of project as it will help ensure against breakage. Both ends are knotted, as you can see in the image, and you can simply tie the ends together now and have a completed necklace or continue along with me. Cut your ends and burn them without impacting your knots if you are done with your necklace.

If you want to continue, then don't cut the ends yet.

Tip #32 - Don't cut and burn near your knot until you're completely done stringing your beads.

You may need the "tail" coming off the knot to tie strands together, so don't cut until your work is finished.

Stringing multiple strands and using findings:

I've repeated the same necklace and strung two more like the first one we did. Now I have three beaded strands of necklaces. In each strand, I added an inch of beads so that they are each a bit longer than the previous one. I did that so we have a *graduated* necklace. Each strand will hang just a tad below the first one.

We can now look at using end caps.

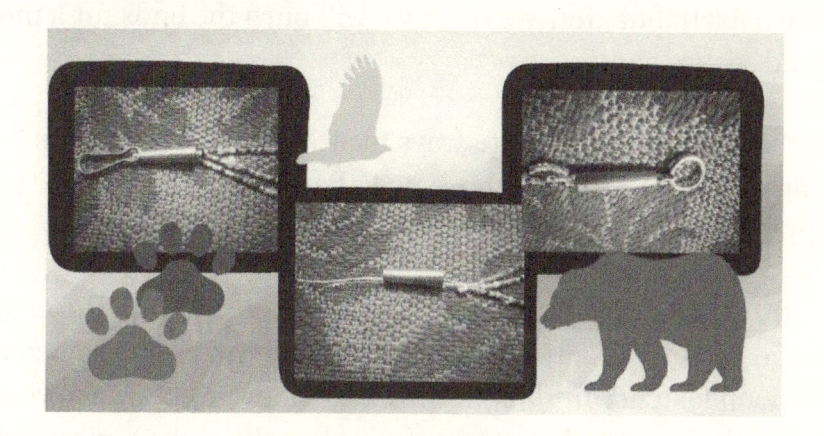

Look at the middle image above. I've taken all three necklaces, tied them together on one end, and strung on an end cap bead. These end caps are longer than some end caps. They can also be used for dangles and other decorative things. But today, they are end caps for your necklace.

Tip #33 - *Use* a decorative bead that is larger for an end cap.

Just make sure your larger bead hole is big enough to pull your finished knots inside like you would an end cap *finding*.

Pull the strings of beads into the end cap and use the leftover threads to tie on a clasp. Mine is pictured above left. It's a very simple spring clasp. In this way, you hide that bigger, ugly knot inside the end cap.

If your large knot from your combined strands comes all the way through your end cap, then thread on a slightly bigger bead before you string the end cap. The bead will stop the knot from coming through and showing. You still have your ending knot showing on the clasp itself, but after we tie it, we will burn the ends for a more tidy and secure ending.

(And there are more intricate ways to attach necklace strands to findings. You can research those now that you know the basic terms and procedures to using some *findings*.)

Gather the other three ends, tie them together, and pull through your end cap in the same manner as the first time. Now you can tie on the loop fastener *finding* in the image above right. Make your knot, cut the loose ends, and carefully burn the ends. Your necklace is complete.

Tip #34 - Be careful of stringing some specialty beads that will be worn near your neck and collar.

They may catch on your hair or buttons on a shirt.

<u>Using Plastic-Coated Wire for stringing beads:</u>

We will begin our project using plastic-coated wire. This wire is usually thin enough to accommodate some of the smaller beads, as well as being very sturdy. Some size 11 beads can be persuaded to go on the wire, and most size 10 beads are easily stranded with coated wire. I recommend this wire where you want lasting strength. It's not authentic Native American beading, but even the Native Americans progressed and used better techniques as materials improved.

The only drawback to using coated wire is that it doesn't have the fluid movement of regular thread. If you use it for a necklace, it tends to hang in a loop and is much more rigid. What you gain in strength, you lose in a more natural movement.

I've decided to make a bracelet because my mother has been wanting me to fix one of hers she bought somewhere. You can see the mix of beads she gave me above left. I added some red white hearts and a few white striped beads. White always shows off other beads really well. I've decided to ditch the broken pieces of chain and simply use the beads. My bracelet will be sturdy using the coated wire.

We begin by pulling out enough wire from its plastic circular "spool" to make a bracelet, plus 2 inches to accommodate attachment to our clasp

Tip #35 - Use a piece of string to measure a person's wrist when making a bracelet, or you will have to guess.

Going larger if guessing is sometimes better than smaller. Guess as well as you are able. Go a bit larger, and in that way, if it's way too big, you will have enough extra wire to simply cut it and perhaps re-attach your clasp.

Generally, when beginning, I like to lay out my beads in a row to see how they should go together and where to space the larger ones.

I laid out one strand and strung the beads. In the picture above, middle, you can see I've already attached my ring *finding*. But you will begin by sliding the end of your wire through the ring, as shown in the middle picture. Your silver crimping bead is on the other side, as shown.

Curl the wire back and slide it back through the bead as in the top right image.

Take your pliers and squeeze the crimping bead as in the top left image. Your wire is now attached. Cut the end of the wire hanging from the crimping bead that's not needed. I try to cut the end as closely as possible because the wire can be pokey and prick your skin when wearing the bracelet.

Now take the beads you've laid out like you want your bracelet and thread them onto the wire. You won't be using a needle for this. The end of the wire will be your needle. What a relief, right? Threading bead needles can be difficult at times.

Tip #36 - If your beads are catching on the end of the wire, simply cut the wire a tiny bit, so the edges of the plastic coating become firm again.

The plastic coating tends to stretch after a while as you thread on your beads.

As shown in the middle image, the last bead you will thread on will be another crimping bead. Thread that end of the wire through your clasp, bend it back to go back through the crimping bead, capturing your clasp. See the top right image. Pull the extra wire and cinch up all your beads before flattening your crimping bead. Squeeze your crimping bead with your pliers, cut the remaining wire, and you have a bracelet.

If you like the look of my mom's finished bracelet with two strands, then simply repeat everything again. You can add several strands to the same *finding,* as shown below.

Now your bracelet is finished. (My mom is going to be thrilled that I finally finished her bracelet.)

You may have guessed that I also used semi-precious *turquoise* chip beads. There are a few larger pieces of turquoise as well. You will see a lot of Native American beadwork using turquoise. It's a traditional choice of bead and color for Native American beadwork.

Tip #37 - Using heavier thread or cord for stringing necklaces is definitely a plus for longevity.

Beadwork is very prone to breakage.

Tip #38 - If your strand of beads is too long, but you really like it, then you can tie the beaded strand into a knot near the lowest point for a nice look.

Just make sure the new knot still accommodates your ability to slide the necklace over your head. I've included a necklace in the beginning illustration that has a knot tied with the strands for an example.

Stringing with cord:

Silken cord makes very beautiful, sturdy necklaces and other adornments. Look at the first picture for this chapter and see the black cord necklace. The hand-blown, peach glass *lamp-work* bead is almost all that's featured, but the simplicity is extremely nice. This lampwork bead is one of the simplest I've seen. Most are much more intricate or blown into shapes.

Tip #39 - It helps to string your beads onto cord; if you use a lighter to burn either end of the cord.

Burning the ends hardens the cord and keeps it from fraying. This way, you will not need a needle to thread your beads. And when tying the knots, they don't fray and come undone. It also leaves cleaner-looking ends.

Use whatever jewelry findings you like to finish your necklace, or simply knot them together. By now, you have an idea of different ways to use jewelry *findings*. And you will now notice the huge variety of them at your local craft store. The choices are almost endless. Fancier ones can add a whole creative touch to your work.

Stringing beads with leather:

Leather can be the most difficult process when stringing beads. They tend not to want to go onto the leather. You can buy leather cord, strands, or cut your own. If you want it very uniform, then buying it should be your choice. However, if you want it to look more like the leather earrings in the picture for this chapter, then you will need to cut your own leather.

These earrings feature a small piece of flatwork sewn onto a circle of leather with the bottom of the circle cut into strands. The strands don't have to be sewn on that way; they are already attached. Then beads were threaded on and held on with a small knot in the leather strand.

But we are going to attempt a necklace made of leather strips, as well as sinew.

Let's begin practicing cutting your own leather with this project.

It's supposed to look very rough, so you don't have to be an expert leatherworker to do this. I chose this project not for the beauty but for practice. Yours will most likely be much more attractive. Think about what you want to include in your necklace before you start. Whatever you use, like my shells, they should have holes large enough to string your leather strands through them.

I've chosen a few basic colors to compliment the shells I picked up on the beach a few years ago. I love beachcombing. With Native American beadwork, you can use them for all kinds of projects. Shells have always been beautiful and sewn into original Native American beadwork, as well as an ornamental addition to clothing. They can easily be substituted for buttons and are very durable. I picked up shells that already had holes in them because you need a diamond bit to drill holes in shells. They are tough.

I also found a Blue Jay feather and decided to include it here.

Tip #40 - Feathers are not legal to use in your beadwork unless they are chicken or turkey feathers.

Native Americans are given leeway, to some degree, for using feathers for their own use if not for sales.

You can buy painted/dyed feathers to look like other eagle, hawk, and owl feathers, or paint your own from chicken or turkey feathers. The painted/dyed feathers can be almost impossible to tell the difference from real ones depending on your supplier.

I've also chosen some semi-precious, black, *onyx* bead chips and a few colors of larger size 8 beads.

In the upper left image, you can see the way to separate your sinew into smaller strands. Simply pull it apart carefully. Or, you can use a full strand if you like. I can't thread the onyx chips onto the leather unless I use a smaller strand and tie it onto my necklace.

Tip #41 - Semi-precious and precious chip beads tend to have very tiny holes.

If you buy larger-sized pieces of the different semi-precious rock beads, your holes may be bigger, but check before you buy.

I will cut a few strands of sinew about ten inches long. Next, we will begin to cut our leather. As you can see in the upper right image, I just have a small piece of leather about the size of my palm.

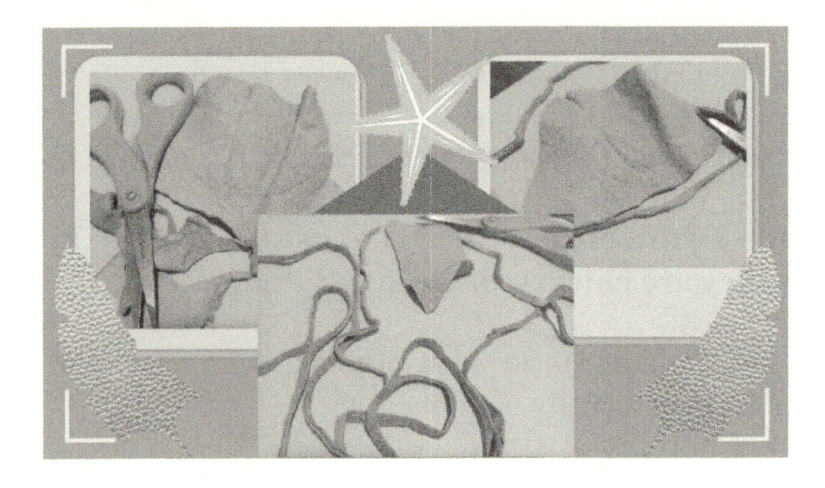

Take your scissors, sharp scissors, and cut off the rougher edges of the leather until it's in somewhat of a circle as in the top left image. Next, you will begin to cut around the outside of the circle, trying to keep the cord as much the same thickness as possible as you go, as in the top right picture. The leather will have a weak spot and can tear if you cut too close.

Tip #42 - Stop and pull on your leather strands as you cut them. Before you begin, check for weak spots that will break as well as any strands you might have purchased already cut.

Just tug enough to stretch the leather strand. This will save you a lot of grief and time as you begin your project. You want strands that won't break easily, so your work is secure. (Mine always tears somewhere, don't feel bad. I have to cut a few before I'm ready to begin.)

We will cut all the way around the circle until the leather strands are long enough for a necklace. Then, hang it around your neck and check the length to where you would like it to hang. Then, before you cut it, pull again and make sure your basic cord will be strong with no weak points. Then, when you get a piece cut long enough without breaking, you will have learned the thickness and process necessary to cut leather cords.

Congratulations! One more skill to add to your growing other ones.

Tip #43 - With leather strands, it doesn't take a large piece of leather for many projects.

Because you don't have to cut in a straight line, you can use leather scraps that are not good for much else.

I've chosen a broken piece of a shell for my centerpiece. I just thought it was pretty. The ocean had worn it smooth where it broke with the motion of the waves and sand. Nature is a wonderful provider.

In the center image, I've taken a smaller piece of leather cord and threaded it through the shell. Now, I will attach it to the main necklace cord in the very middle. Look at the top left to see how I tie the two ends together to attach the shell. It will look like the top right when you tighten down the knot. In this way, you will have the shell securely tied, with two tails hanging down.

We want the extra cords, so don't cut them!

Here is a great spot to stop and dip all the leather strands you will be using into warm water. Surprise! I know you didn't see that coming. But leather will "set" after you're done. And we will begin twisting the strands for a more interesting finished product. It will help it look worn and not brand newly cut.

Tip #44 - When leather strands are wet, you can tighten down your knots better, and they stay more secure.

Damp leather also holds a shape from twisting it or forming it—as in the art of *leather tooling*.

You will see the effects of the leather being twisted versus left undone by the end. Either way is fine for your project, but I'm supposed to give you the expert advice here, so take it or leave it. After that, it's up to you how you like it. This is your creation!

We don't twist the sinew for visual effect. I do have to twist the end of my sinew to get it to thread through those small holes in my onyx beads, though.

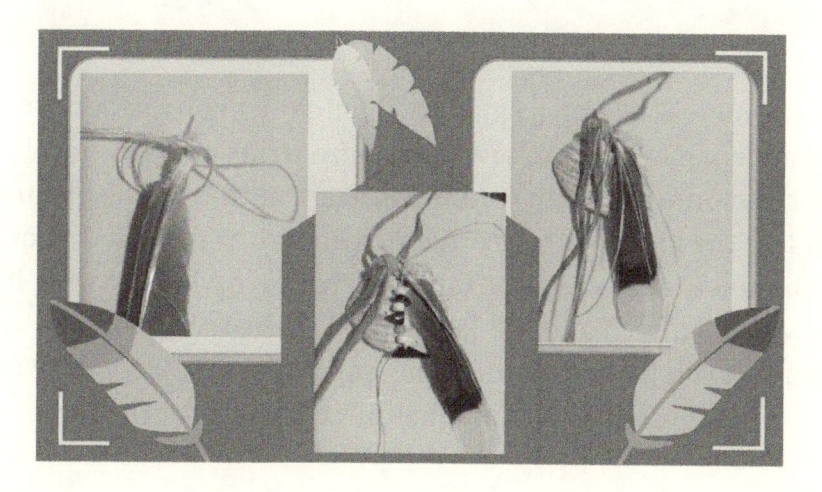

Take a piece of your sinew, and tie it onto your feather very tightly, as in the upper left image. Then tie it through the shell's hole along with the leather cord there. In the upper right image, you can see that we now have a lot going on around the shell.

Let's use a piece of your sinew hanging down and thread on a few beads like in the middle picture. Knot the bottom of the sinew and make sure your beads can't fall off. I use one of the onyx beads at the bottom of the beads because its hole is so small, which helps hold the other beads on. The onyx stone won't slip over the knot as easily.

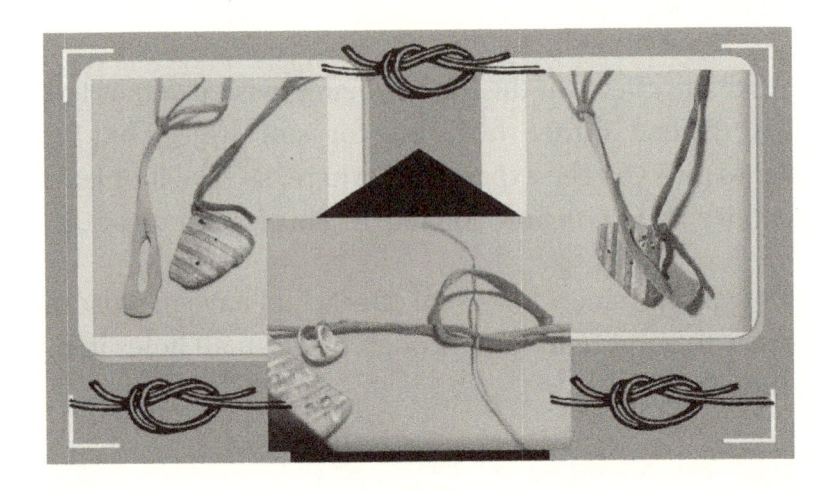

Now I've simply tied on a small shell onto the main leather cord in the middle picture above. I will add more strips of sinew now by tying them onto the main cord. Look again at the middle picture. Then I tie the main leather cord into a knot over the sinew knot so that the sinew doesn't have a tendency to move while wearing it. Finally, I will attach another larger shell above the small shell along the cord. It will be tied on the same way as the first large shell in the middle. And I will also add another piece of sinew at the same place.

We will end up with the large shell in the middle, one smaller one tied onto the leather cord two inches above that, and another large shell tied on two inches above that, just like the first one in the middle. It gives you a larger shell in the middle, a small shell on both sides, and then a middle-sized shell on both sides of the centerpiece. We now have several pieces of sinew hanging off the main cord, as well as several pieces of sinew hanging down from shells we tied on.

I add beads onto the sinew here and there as it looks good to me. Put as many beads into the necklace as you like. I only chose to use a few shells, but you can add them how you like. And other things work just as well as shells. Use decorative beads or whatever you like that looks beautiful to you.

But we need to figure out how we will end this necklace, so look at the top left image. I've tied on a piece of shell to one end and tied on a piece of leather cord with part of the circle of leather left at the end. In that circle of leather, I've cut a hole just wide enough for my piece of shell to slip through.

Now we have fashioned a rudimentary clasp that matches the theme of our necklace. A large bead also works well for a catch through your leather fob. I simply chose to keep my shell theme going for this necklace. You can see how it catches in the top right image.

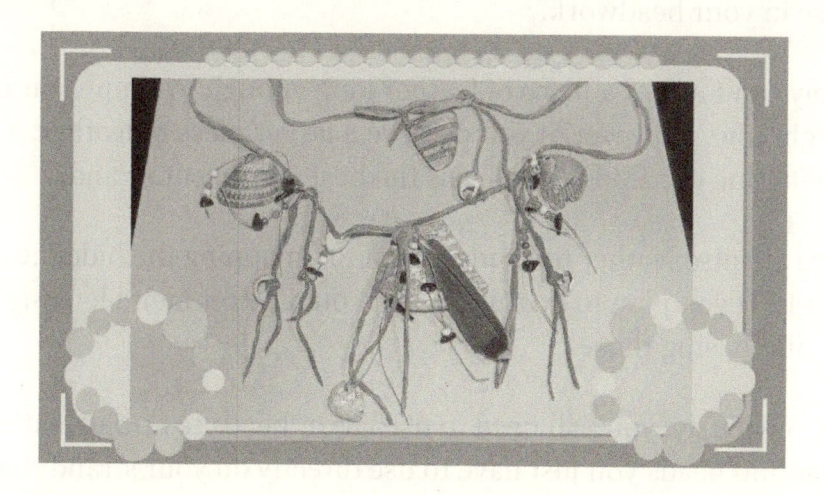

My rudimentary leather necklace ended up looking like this. I'm very curious to know how yours looks. That's the only sad part about being the writer instead of the reader.

These raw-looking necklaces are really more attractive when worn. It's also a great project as a gift for a man.

You can see in the image the effects of twisting the leather, the way the shells were set into the main cord, and how I added in other beads for variety. It's a very rough and natural-looking necklace that works really well with a leather jacket or matching a pair of moccasins or leather boots. And it gives you an outlet to show off the treasures you've collected from our Great Spirit, who provides us with so many gifts in this world.

Tip #45 - Choose leather that is not coated with glossy or glittery coatings.

Some of these types of leather will be great in a few projects, but the treated leather without coatings is much easier and more versatile to use in your beadwork.

Rarely can I afford a piece of leather long enough to simply cut in a straight line. However, if you do have a larger piece of leather, a straight line cut along the edge is the best way to cut strands.

There are also leather tools made just for stripping the hide into strands. If you plan to do this a lot, I would recommend looking into purchasing those.

And, obviously, you will need to use larger beads to strand leather. If you find beads you just have to use directly on your strand that don't easily slide on, you can use a beading awl designed for this purpose. You will insert the awl into the bead and twist lightly. It's easy to break glass beads, so take it slow. Other beads will be more cooperative. But, if they're thin, you're making them vulnerable to breaking.

You can either string your beads onto a leather cord in a solid row or string on a bead in a certain place along the strand by making a simple knot before and behind it. I also gave you a great shortcut using pieces of sinew tied into your work. The sinew will give you more choices in smaller beads to use as well as blending in with the leather.

Tip #46 - *Leather is one of the best materials to use in Native American beadwork.*

The edges don't fray when using it for flatwork and finishing beadwork, and you can use a single piece for several kinds of projects.

Chapter Review:

- We learned different ways to string beads using beading thread, cord, coated wire, or leather and sinew.
- Tying off ends and using findings to finish our work is explained and visually shown as part of finishing a necklace or bracelet.
- Working with stripping leather and using sinew for a practical application was shown from start to finish.

Chapter 4: A Day for Daisy Chains

Instructions:

This is one of the simplest stitches in Native American beadwork. Many times young girls are taught this to begin beading. It's no accident. It allows you to use your needle, pass through a bead a second time, and experience how beadwork feels holding it while in the process.

And have no fear, if worse comes to worst, and you can't quite get this, no worries. There are a lot of stitches to come that might make more sense to you.

But you will rock this! I've provided expert diagrams just to help you out. :))

To begin:

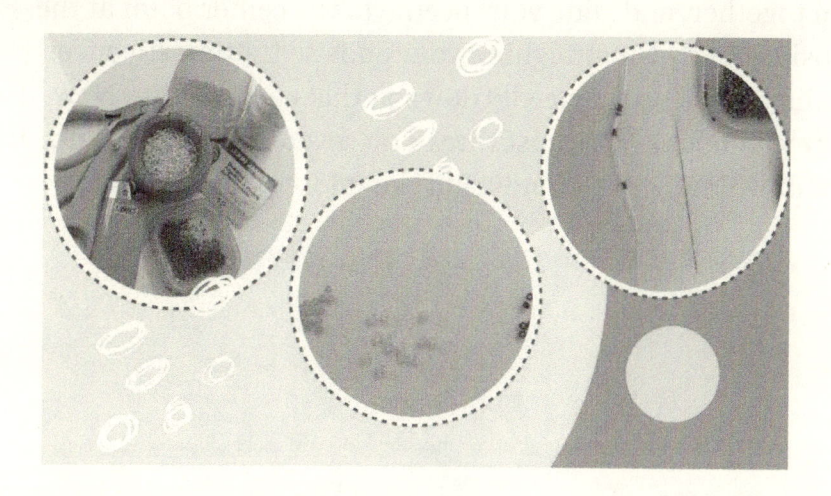

The photo above shows you the materials needed for a Daisy Chain project. I have selected the petals/pink with a size 11 bead. (The pink ones are a bit larger than the others.) The middle of the flower will be orange, and the leaf separating the flowers is a dark green. These beads are size 12, and there's no glisten to the beads. You can see the pink beads are very glossy looking, matching my idea of a flower petal.

To begin, you will thread a needle with about an arm's length of beading thread. I'm using a size 12 needle, and it will be large enough for the size 11 beads as well. Remember, they are larger than size 11 beads, so our needle will work for both sizes.

Tip #47 - Buy size 12 needles as your standard for most of your beginning beadwork.

It will work for the size 11 and 12 beads, and some sized 13 beads, too, if they are made with good "open" holes.

As you thread on your needle, take the two ends of the string, hold them together, and slide your needle to the center point at the opposite end. Next, straighten your ends so they mostly meet together and keep the needle down at that center point. Now, don't worry yet about a knot; just thread on seven green beads and slide them down to the loose ends. But don't lose them!

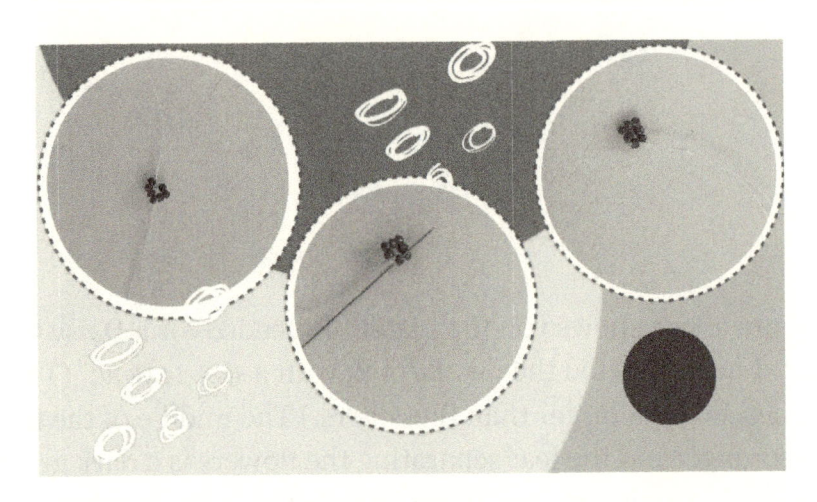

Tie the beads on into a circle as in the first picture. Make sure your knot is secure, then cut and burn the end so that it looks like the top right picture.

Tip #48 - Hide your knots where you can.

It shows a higher level of expertise and a "cleaner" finish when you hide your knots in your beadwork.

Yes! We can learn to be an expert beader from the first project.

Here is your first lesson on hiding knots:

You will pick up the bead next to the knot and push your needle through it to hide your knot. As your string follows, you can pull that knot into the bead itself, as in the middle image above. You may feel it "pop" into the bead. How slick is that?

Don't tug too hard. If the knot doesn't go through, your knot may be a bit large. Practice making smaller knots as you go through this book. And, sometimes the knots go all the way through, and you see them anyway. No worries! We will simply practice and continue on. A knot or two isn't a big deal. You will get better and better.

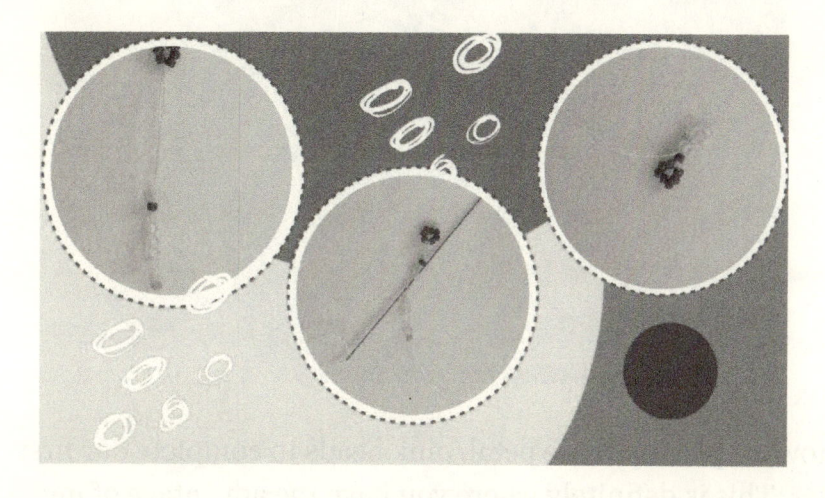

Now you're saying, "Hey, I tried, and my knot just slid through, and you can still see it!" Well, that happens sometimes. Don't worry. Look at the top left circle; you can sort of see my knot too. And we will begin anyway. Pick up one green bead, four pink beads, and one orange bead. Slide them down to the green circle and thread your needle through the first pink bead you threaded on. Thread your needle back into the top of the bead, not the bottom! Next, look at the middle image. This is important if you don't want to wrestle with your flowers. (Aren't you glad I included helpful pictures? I know!)

Pull the thread through and slide the orange bead around so that it looks like the top right circle. You will do this move over and over, so get comfortable with it. Don't worry if your beads won't stay one way or another; they will resolve themselves as we go. Just try to cinch them down and slide them as close to the green circle as you can so you won't have a lot of string showing in between the flowers. We want all the beads tight against each other with little to no string showing.

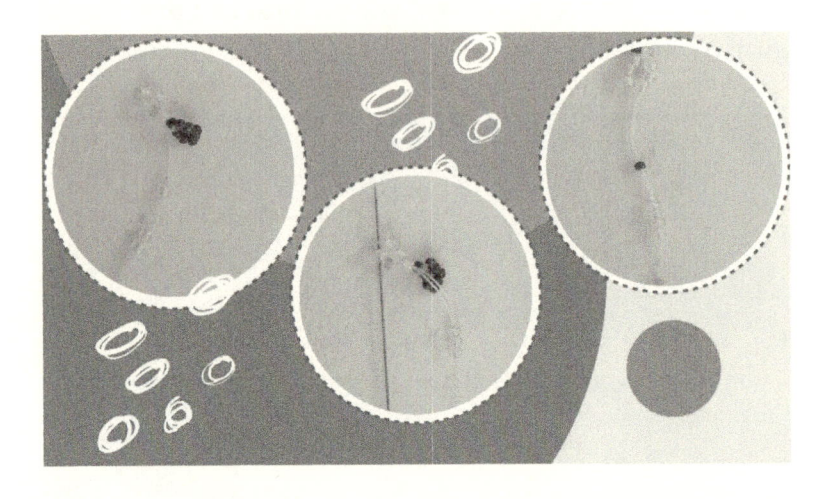

So now we pick up three petal/pink beads to complete our first flower. This is definitely where you have the advantage of my illustration. First, guide your needle as shown in the middle circle. Next, you will go through the bottom of the fourth pink bead you originally put on. This is your first really complicated threading that will get you accustomed to holding your thread and needle and beadwork, all at the same time. I know it can feel very awkward, hence the practice with this Daisy Chain.

Pull your thread through as in the top right circle. And you have now completed your first flower, as shown. Thread on one green, four petal/pink, and one orange bead. This is the very same as you did on the first flower.

Tip #49 - Look up some basic knots to learn the "square knot" and others.

A square knot or even double square knot is what I mostly use in beadwork. However, there are a lot of varieties of knots that are more secure, so you be the judge and enjoy using whatever knot you like.

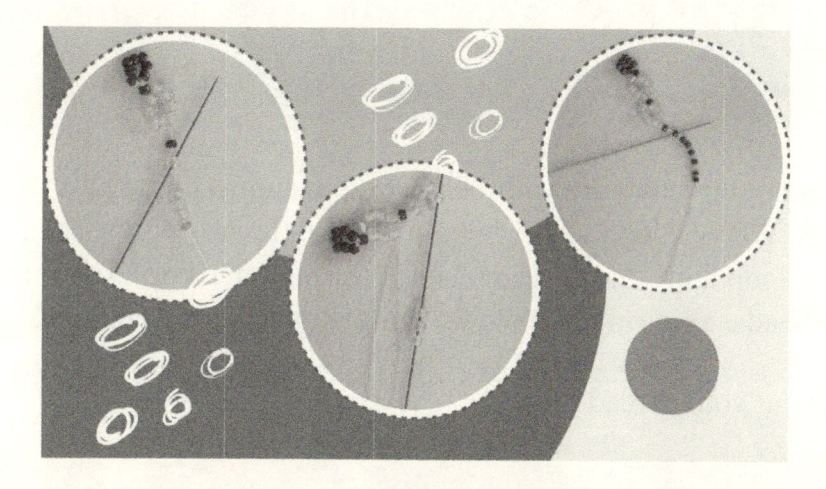

Now you can see the same steps as the first flower. Follow the circle images to repeat a second flower for your Daisy Chain. And after that, we will end this chain as we began it, like in the top right circle. Thread on eight green beads, then go through the second bead from the bottom as shown.

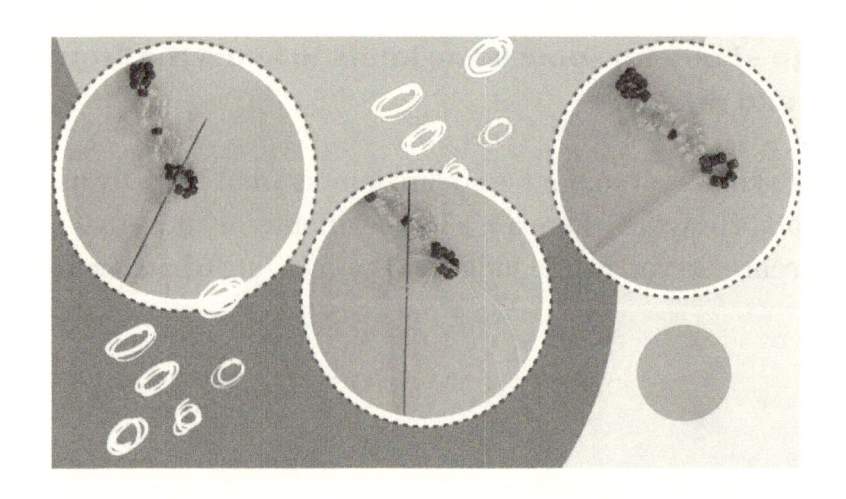

Tie a knot directly onto your beadwork, as shown in the first two circles. You will loop your string under the thread holding the beads, loop it around and come back through the loop to tie it to your beads. You can do this twice for a double knot if you like.

Don't cut your thread off yet!

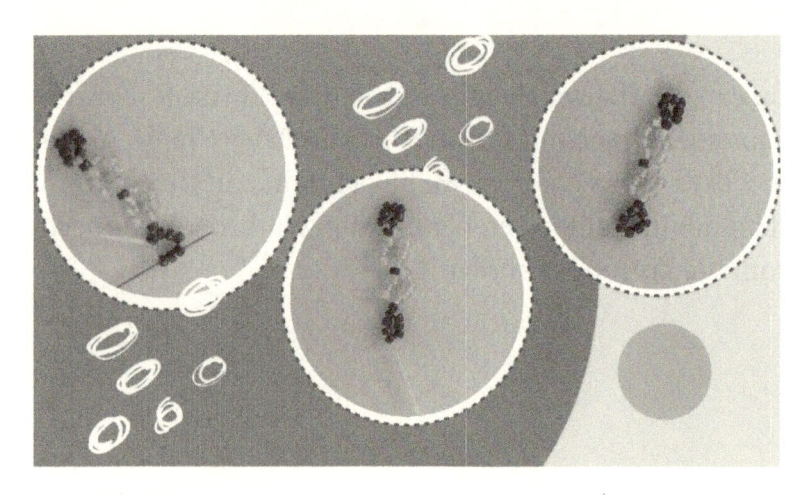

Here we will also practice hiding your knot yet again. This not only gives you a cleaner piece of work, but it actually helps your knots to keep from unraveling.

Simply thread your needle through the three beads beside your knot, as in the top left image. Now your needle is coming out of the bottom of the green circle of beads shown in the middle image. Pull just a tad and see if your knot will slide inside a bead. Did you feel it "pop" inside? Just right. Here is where we imagine you have a whole Daisy Chain beaded behind that green beaded circle.

Now is when you can cut your thread and burn the ends.

Burning the ends as a habit is just called *insurance*.

Your work should look similar to the top right circle. I knew you could do it! You have now become a Native American beader. Yes, it's not hard; it's fun!

Tip #50 - When you sit down to bead, be aware that chairs with arms will catch your thread as you work.

Pick areas that are free of items or furniture that could catch on your thread. You should also sit far enough away from other people to avoid entangling your thread or stabbing them with a needle as you pull your thread out through a piece of beadwork. It happens! : (((

Adding String to Your Project to Continue Beading:

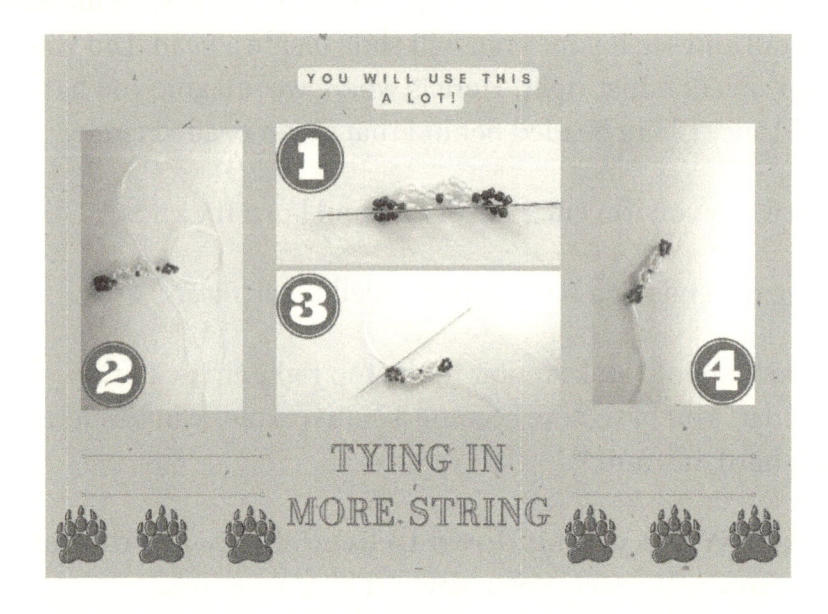

Keep this page tagged in case you need it down the line. It's a constant thing you will need to do among all the stitches.

Pick a spot along your beadwork to add thread and slide your needle between the beads as in image #1. Pull your thread through until you just leave a tail and tie on the knot as in image #2. I've shown you how to make one knot, but there are countless ones you can use. For example, if you make a circle like the above and actually slide your needle around and through the loop two times, it's a much more secure knot. But you can also repeat the image in circle two, and you will have a square knot.

Cinch your knot down tight and thread your needle through beads next to the knot-like image #3. Then, go through one more and pull the knot into the beads as you can.

Thread your needle through the beads to make your way to the spot you want to pick up and continue your work as in #4. It is helpful to tie the knot close by, but not necessary. The more you go through beads after a knot, the safer your beadwork will stay.

Now cut the tail that's left from the knot, and burn the ends. Carefully! You don't want to burn through the original beadwork.

Done. I suggest you try not to get impatient with all this needlework. It will begin flowing like a crystal clear stream in the summertime soon enough. Then, you will forget your original awkwardness.

Chapter Review:

- This chapter explained why we begin our first beading stitch, the Daisy Chain.
- We learned how to create a Daisy Chain using three colors of seed beads.
- We were shown how to hide our knots inside a bead, so our work is tidier.
- Tying in a new piece of thread is explained for this project and ongoing projects to come.

Chapter 5: The Brick Stitch

Here is a simple project creating a brick-stitched earring. I've provided a sample of a basic Brick Stitch pattern made with Brick Stitch pattern paper and filled it in with my map colors. As you can see, the earring is much more beautiful than the pattern shows.

I added simple dangles not shown in the pattern for you to finish your piece. You won't be able to see the dangles on Brick Stitch pattern paper as they don't fit like the beaded work they are attached to. But you can design your dangles using loom pattern paper if you want to. I've given you a way to simply count out a pattern as we go. But there are many dangles created where the pattern for the dangles is graduated and creates a whole design to go with the original Brick Stitch work. Check it out online. It's usually created in a V pattern or an upside-down V using different colored beads for effect.

Here, you will get to practice Brick Stitch, adding thread, tying off your thread into the beadwork, and adding dangles to the body of your work. Lots to learn! And all of it will aid you in the upcoming chapters.

Here is a picture of the supplies needed to make our earrings, as well as the first two steps in the beadwork. First, I chose a darker bead, a gunmetal mix-hued bead, for the main body. I chose the dark bead to see the white thread more easily in the pictures. The other beads are solid light pink, as well as a darker metallic pink bead.

Tip #51 - I usually pull out my thread to the same length as my arm to begin beading.

It usually gives me a bit extra if needed. Of course, if you need to add more thread, you can. But more thread than an arm-length is harder to handle and likes to knot up at any and every occasion you let it.

Brick Stitch is the one time I usually don't use a double thread. It's easier for you to use a single strand for this. Also, doubling your thread can sometimes make your beadwork too stiff by the end of a brick-stitched project.

I begin by threading the needle, then threading on two beads of our bottom layer of the project shown on the pattern. The "bottom" is the widest part of the pattern. It's helpful with Brick Stitch to always begin at the widest place as a foundation. Your pattern will naturally begin to decrease with Brick Stitch, which is easier than adding in beads to a row.

Tip #52 - It's imperative that you start from one corner/side of your pattern and always follow from that direction for every line afterward.

This ensures the pattern is counted out correctly, especially in the more complex stitch techniques.

As you can see from the middle image above, we are beginning with the bottom row, which is all the dark gunmetal beads. Look at your pattern in the top left image to see the bottom row of beads. It's the widest part of the pattern as well. Make sure to keep checking the pattern as we go to be sure you are following it correctly.

String on two of the dark beads, and don't lose them at the bottom as we don't have a knot tied yet.

After the beads are threaded on, slide them towards the end of the thread and tie them onto the end, as shown in the top right image. Flatten them out, and don't tie them too tightly together. You want them to lie flat, as shown with the holes up and the beads beside each other. You can see it in the top right image. If they are too tight, they will look more like the middle picture before they were tied.

Cut and burn the end of the thread hanging off, not attached to your needle.

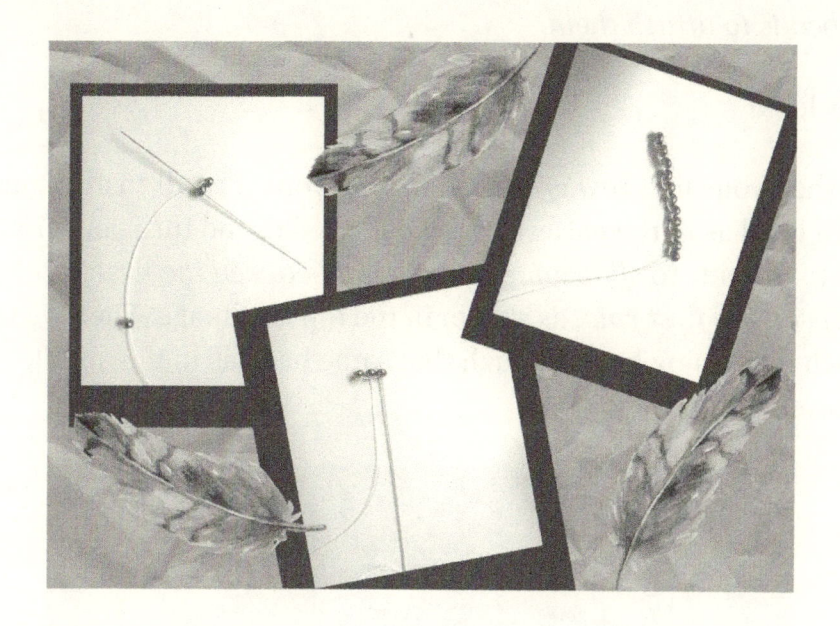

Now we will proceed along the first row of our Brick Stitch. After securing the first two beads with our first knot, we thread on another bead and enter the second bead from the end to add our third bead. Come back through that third bead as shown in the middle picture before adding another one on. Now you are ready to repeat by adding on one bead at a time until you have the total count shown on your pattern. There will be 11 dark beads for the first row of your pattern completed.

Your line of bricks (beads) will look like the upper right picture. As you can see, they are a bit lopsided here and there. Not to worry! *The first row is always, always, the most difficult in most of the beadwork patterns*. As you add the next layer of bricks (beads), you will find that they straighten out and behave.

This is important to remember:

In the first row, you will be sewing the beads together, *but all the rest of the rows, you will simply be picking up the thread between the beads to attach them.*

Let's look!

So when your first row is done, don't cut your thread! Instead, just add a bead as in the pattern onto your needle, and turn your first row to the side to *slide under the thread between the first two beads on the first row*, as shown in the top left image. Then we will attach it by going back through that same bead as in the middle picture.

Make sure you continue to go under the threads on the same side of your first row, or it will get very confusing. Your rows will naturally fit the bead between like bricks as you attach them, hence the name of the Brick Stitch. Slide the bead down until it's snug against the first row as in the upper right picture.

I know, I know! Your thread wants to knot up, and the beads don't want to behave!

Part of beadwork is learning to hold the beadwork a certain way as you go. I can't explain how this will work for you as an individual, but **don't give up**! Unraveling knotted thread, holding your beadwork a certain way, and cinching down beads are all tactical things your body will show you as you go. Just breathe and be patient. The more you practice, the better it gets.

And here we see the second bead being added to the first row. You will notice it is pink according to our pattern. And just in case you weren't sure if you are doing it correctly, I've added these pictures to clear things up. Repeat adding a bead at a time until your second row is done. You may notice that your beads naturally follow the pattern and decrease by one bead in each row. They simply fit this way and naturally follow this particular pattern. However, we will also learn how to add a bead if you need to, further down.

The upper right picture shows you how your beadwork should be progressing as you finish the second row. Again, look at the pattern and your beads to be sure you have put on the correct colored beads. It's much easier to fix now than later.

If you need to undo your work, just take off your needle and pull your thread through everything back out the way it went on until you are at the point of the mistake. Then, thread your needle back on, fix it, and catch up! But, hey, we all get to "catch up" sometimes with lots of stuff in life—no big deal.

My beadwork is looking a little lumpy, you say? Well, yes, it is. Here is an excellent example of the difference beads make if they are a bit smaller or larger. My beads were all size 11, but you can see the manufacturer differences even among the same size. But it's OK. They aren't too different, so we can proceed. However, if you have a different kind of project sensitive to this, or you are a bit of a perfectionist, then be sure to check your beads closely when mixing them together in the same project.

After you have followed your pattern *religiously*, added all the layers until the very top bead is attached; then, we will add on seven of your darker beads so we can use an earring *finding* hanger to attach appropriately.

This isn't in the pattern! So sorry. This is just experienced beader stuff I'm throwing in for your best-looking finished earring. This technique also helps your earring hang straight. I will show you another way to do this that's somewhat complicated in a project coming up.

I thread on seven dark beads to match my outline color, then go back into the bead on top and down through one side of the beadwork so that you come out at the bottom where you started. The middle image is the best to view this.

And in the top right image, you see what we call the finished main body of work for your Brick Stitch earring. And, as you can see, the beadwork has resolved itself into a nice solid brick wall of beads. They tend to straighten out as you go.

Your ending brick-work project should look similar to the upper right picture. I knew you could do it!

Increasing Beads on a New Row of Brick Stitch

This is easy! Now that you've got the hang of Brick Stitch, adding a bead onto a row is not so difficult. I will show you how to add to the front of the row and to the back of the row. If you need to add a whole row onto a pattern, it will need to increase by one bead, and it's simply like the above pictures.

We will increase by two beads, one on each end, so we have an even number of beads to attach our dangles. The bead attaching at the end of the row will be different from how you added the first two beads.

As you can see in the upper left image, coming out of your first row of Brick Stitch, you will add two beads onto the row. The second illustration shows how you attach the two beads. I'm sure it looks familiar, doesn't it? You simply skip going through the first bead; it will attach with the other one anyway, without going through them both.

Now, continue to add beads the same way as in the first row above it. One bead at a time until you come to the end of the row. Attach your last bead to the row like normal, and you will be able to count out eleven beads on the row. Pick up one more dark bead, thread your needle up into *the last bead on the first row above where you are working,* and thread it back down into the bead you are adding onto the end of the row. Cinch it down, and you will now be done.

Now you will have 12 beads in the row you just added. It will allow you to attach six dangles. Look below at the finished beadwork to see the 12 beads added to the original row of ten. We added one extra bead on either end.

If you don't want to learn this yet, you can simply add five dangles instead of six and be done. But some of your patterns in the future may need beads added or reduced. I recommend trying to do this now. Take it at your pace.

Tip #53 - When adding dangles, I recommend using a double strand of thread for durability.

A single strand of thread is simply asking for breakage. Dangles move a lot and are susceptible to catching on collars and buttons on clothing as you move.

Now, with your thread coming out the bottom where we ended, you should add dangles. Next, we will tie off your work and add a double strand of thread, which will show you how to add thread, hide knots, and progress.

So, tie a knot at the bottom of your beadwork, run the needle up into the next bead over, pull it up into the bead if you can, and cut and burn the end. This way, your ending knot is hidden. The knots at the bottom of your work here tend to be hidden within the dangles as well, so it's not so visible in this application.

Take another piece of thread about arm's length and double it. Thread on your needle, slide the needle to the middle of the piece of thread and knot the two ends together. Then cut and burn the ends from the knot. It should look like the picture in the upper left image. Easy, right? Of course, you've done this already! :))

Follow the picture in the upper right, and thread your needle a few beads up from the bottom row, the needle facing downward to the bottom of the beadwork. You will slide the needle in, and as the knot catches, you will pull your thread all the way through. It will look like the bottom picture. Do you see the knot?

We can get rid of that problem knot. You simply tug the knot into the hole of the bead to hide it. I know I've already covered this, but sometimes it takes me a few times to remember directions and "get it." I want everyone to understand how simple it is to do a really great job with their knots and beadwork.

Now we are ready to attach dangles with a doubled strand of thread. Dangles lose a bit of their movement if the thread is doubled but gain longevity. It's your decision as you progress.

Tip #54 - Dangles can take a lot more beads compared to your main body of work in many projects.

Plan the number of beads needed for the added dangles before starting the stitch work. You won't want to run out of certain colors involved for your dangles.

With your new piece of doubled thread coming out the bottom of your beadwork, as in the top left image, you will begin the dangles.

Thread on one black, one metallic, one pink, one metallic, then five black, three metallic, 15 pink, three metallic, five black, one metallic, one pink, one metallic, five black, one metallic, one pink, one metallic, and finally, one black bead.

Phew! Did you get all that?

The top left picture shows you how it will look as you thread them on. Go to the top right example to see how we attach our dangle. You simply go up with your needle into the next bead on the bottom row. Then pull your thread all the way through.

As you can see, the way you add beads to a dangle creates a whole pattern of their own by the time you are done. Refer back to the first diagram if you like to see how this creates your ongoing pattern.

Now, look at our bottom picture and go back down into the next bead on the first row of your beadwork. Then thread on the same pattern of beads, and repeat. You will end up with six full dangles.

Tip #55 - Typically, I thread on three sets of 15 beads to make one dangle.

It's a general theme, but it gives me a basic guide when designing my dangles. This way, I can also count out an estimate of 45 beads for each dangle and figure out how many of each bead color I may need. It also usually makes a nice length for a dangle with plenty of movement. And I usually use a lighter color for the bottom of the dangle, but it's just my own visual preference.

Here is where you can begin to incorporate your own design for the dangles as well, even as a beginner. I've tried to give you an example only while you learn. As you design your own projects, you'll find more satisfaction, and it's unique to you if you create your own patterns, which makes it very special.

Once more, here we thread our needle up into the beadwork when finished with the dangles. Tie off by picking up the thread of the beadwork as in the upper left image and making a knot on that as in the upper right image.

After the knot is made, you will slide your needle into the beads above it and pull your thread through. Next, tug the knot into the bead above it, "pop," cut the ends of your thread, burn, and you are now done.

Now you can repeat all of these directions for Brick Stitch to finish your first *pair* of Brick Stitch earrings. I hope you wear them proudly; you deserve it.

Here you can see your earrings with the appropriate *findings* attached. There are several styles of earring *findings*, but these are the simplest, where you just slide the earring onto the *finding*. You now see why we made a loop of beads at the top.

Tip #56 - Be aware that the metal in earrings is especially important when you choose them.

Many people are sensitive to what kinds of metals they can tolerate. The better the metal, the more expensive your *findings* will be. Your choice in this is especially important for earrings. In other jewelry pieces, it may not be as relevant.

Think about the Statue of Liberty. She was designed with a metal that would wear over time into a beautiful green. This wasn't the original color of the metal. Yikes! But we don't probably want green metal in our findings over time.

Good silver findings are very prevalent. Gold earring hoops and posts can be purchased as needed. Check out the variety of findings, but don't be persuaded just by the design. Check the metal for quality as well where needed.

Chapter Review:

- The way to weave beads using the Brick Stitch was illustrated and explained.
- We were given a practical example to follow so we could learn to create a set of earrings using the Brick Stitch.
- Adding dangles is explained and illustrated.
- Finishing our project with jewelry *findings* is shown for these earrings.
- Increasing our row of beads by adding beads is explained and illustrated for Brick Stitch.

Chapter 6: Mother Earth Medallion

We have a special treat now. I have another stitch that works well for earrings as well as other applications. Mostly I've seen this sewn into earrings. However, I've used it to make large barrettes and also as a bottom for a medicine pouch.

Tip #57 - Don't get your mind stuck on using your new stitches for just these sample projects.

Remember, you're learning to become an expert like me. So let your mind open as you learn.

The medallion can be the simplest yet most difficult for some people. It's the repetitiveness of it that confuses people. You would think this would be the easiest part, just repeat what you did the first time, but I'm going to give you a real-life example that happened to me while I was making these for you! Imagine it; your expert beader still finds this troubling.

Here are our *fire colors* medallion earrings. And they are finished and beautiful. But, if you look closely, you'll see one is smaller. That's your first clue!

I did not end up with matching medallions, so beware. Don't underestimate these beauties. The only thing I did differently was to begin my earrings with 12 beads, and on the next one, I used only 10 in the middle. You can see the difference it made. You get a whole different pattern of stars in the middle beads.

While using either 12 or 10, to begin with, is totally acceptable, now I will have to make a match for each one if I want to use them. I knew one friend who I taught to make these, and she ended up with ten different sets of earrings before she got them all to match. However, she really knew how to make them really well after that. And she was already an expert beader.

While color combinations can be difficult to follow with these, and that is how she got so confused, using a single color is the most difficult. Some combinations can look like stained glass windows, and others can even mimic a snowflake. Nevertheless, you can make some beautiful pieces with this stitch.

Let's just begin and enjoy the beautiful results! I think it's easier than Brick Stitch, and unless you draw it out free-hand, there is no pattern paper for this. I've chosen the beautiful Native American *fire colors*, which are very traditional in all native beadwork. The chapter image shows you the different colors of beads you will need.

I am using an arm's length of thread and doubled it. Pull your needle to the middle of your thread, and don't knot it yet. We will begin by threading on 12 turquoise-colored beads. I've chosen all "flat" colored beads that have no tri-cuts or see-through, *opaque* look—very straightforward beads for our medallion.

Slide the beads to the bottom ends of your thread and tie them into a circle, as shown in the left illustration. Cut the ends of the threads, burn, and go through a bead or two and pull your knot inside a bead, "pop," to hide. Can you see my knot in the image to the right? Barely.

And so, where your thread ends up coming out from this circle of beads, you will thread on three more tortoise beads and **skip** one bead to slide your needle into the next bead. Now you will have skipped one bead and gone into the next one with three beads attaching to form the first leg of your "star." This will show up in the middle of your medallion when you're finished with this layer.

You will go around the original little circle of beads doing the same thing, skipping one bead around the circle next to where your needle comes out and going into the next bead on the circle after you thread three more beads onto your needle. See, you will make arms of your tiny star all the way around. It will be six sets of three beads for each arm of the star. Look at the image on the left to see the bead skipped between each place you go in and out.

After you get your turquoise star formed, we will begin the next layer with dark green beads. You begin by sliding your needle to the top of one star, as seen in the left image. Next, thread on five green beads, and go to the next "point" of the star beside the one you came from. This is a bit simpler.

Continue threading on five green beads and going only through the tip bead of each leg of the star. You will do this six times as well. It will make six half loops of green beads between the turquoise star. Your ending work should look like the image on the right.

Go through four of your green beads on one of the half loops to come out, as shown on the right side image. We will be using the middle three green beads of each half-loop now. For the first star, we used the tip bead. Now, we will use the middle three green beads to go through when attaching our new layer.

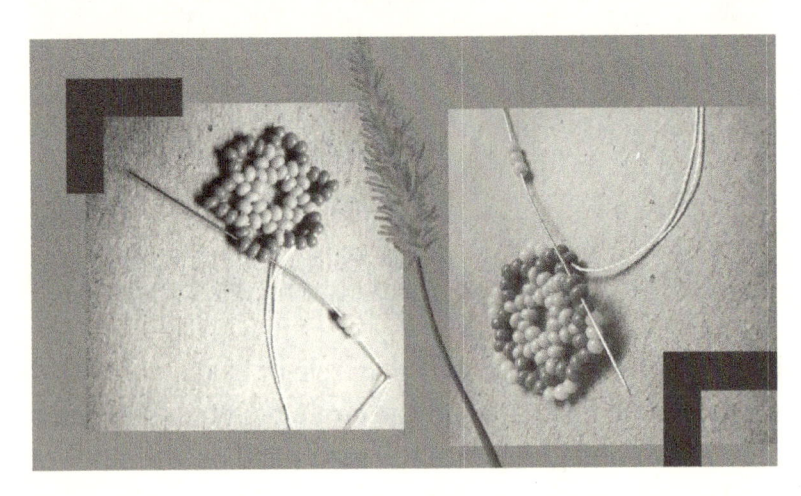

Take up three yellow beads. And jump over to the next loop of green beads. Go into the middle three and out the other side. Now your first loop of yellow is attached. Continue around the same way to form the first layer of yellow. It gets a bit complicated in this layer, so I kept it the same color. Take a breath when you end and thread your needle to the middle of the first loop of yellow. We will be picking up the middle bead only again now.

See, this gets busy! But you can do it. You have an expert guide with illustrations. Be a brave warrior, and you will have victory.

Now we continue. You will have your thread coming out of the middle bead of one of the yellow loops to begin; thread on three more yellow beads. Jump over to the middle bead of the green loop next to your yellow loop. Go through the middle bead only on the green and then thread on three more yellow beads. Jump to the next yellow loop and pick up the middle bead only. Thread on three more yellow beads, jump down to the next green loop, and go through the middle bead of that loop. We go all the way around like this until you have a double layer of yellow beads in sets of three all the way around. You can see the layer in the left image.

This may seem a bit hard to keep track of at first. Take your time. Let yourself enjoy this. Breathe and put it down for a minute. Be kind to yourself while beading. We want to develop a love for this work, so it's OK to learn at a leisurely pace.

Tip #58 - Put on some Native American flute music or the wonderful drumming CDs that feature Native American artists.

Some of the music is very soothing and inspiring to get you "in the mood" while beading.

Your earring is beginning to look beautiful. You could stop after the intricate double layer, but then we would miss the FIRE! I know you want ALL these beautiful colors.

In the top left image, you can see your thread coming out of the tip of one of the loops of yellow. We will pick up the middle bead on the tip of this yellow layer now all the way around.

Thread on five orange beads. These orange beads have a glaze on them that is different than the other flat ones. Think of the colors like buying paint in the hardware store. This orange has a "gloss." But the flat orange would work as well. So I simply grabbed the first great-looking orange beads that I saw.

We will go into the very next loop of yellow, picking up the middle bead only. One loop of orange is now on. Continue around until you have all 12 orange loops. Now you see, we are back to the number 12 instead of six. Anytime you add a double row like the yellow, it opens up your beadwork a lot wider. Be careful, though, not to use a double row too often.

BTW, you can add as many loops, layers, to these as you like. You simply have to try them out to see how they should count out so your bead medallion will lay flat. If you use too many double rows or too many beads between loops, it will get "wavy," like lacy crocheting. But I haven't found it helpful in beading.

Your layer of orange loops should turn out like the right image above. Thread through one loop of orange to come out of the middle bead because we are going to repeat going through the tip of each orange loop bead again. Hey, you say, "I've done that, no sweat!". Yes, you have. Now we will just do it with the fire red beads for the last and final layer of our medallion.

Great job so far! If you're still with me, then you've done the hardest part.

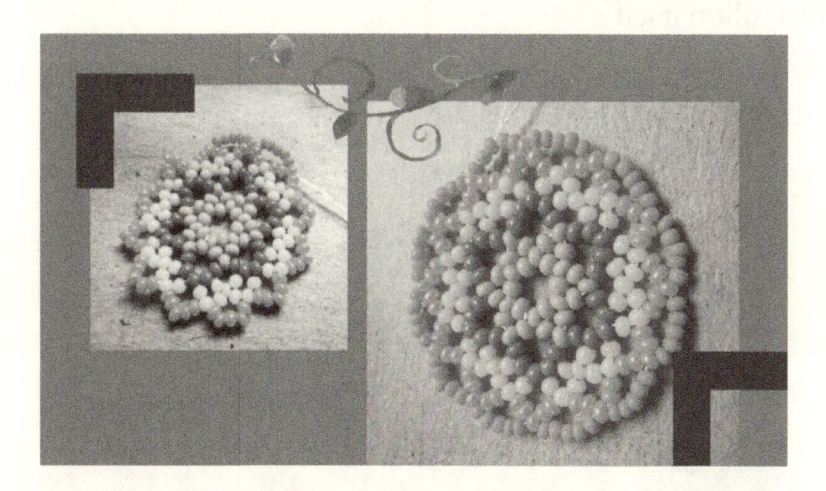

Tip #59 - If you're adding thread to an ongoing project, choose the lightest colored bead to tie it on beside if you are using white thread

The closer your threaded knot is to the color of the bead you're tying beside, the better you can hide it.

Now, add five fire red beads onto your thread, jump to the middle of the next orange loop, pick up the middle bead, add five fire red beads and repeat. You will add five fire red beads all the way around between each orange loop.

Your medallion is actually finished. But, we need to have a "topper" added to make sure your medallion hangs correctly on an earring *finding*. Because these medallions are circular, they tend to try to curl while hanging. But, lucky you, your expert guide knows how to resolve this problem already.

Because they are prone to curling in, that is also why we doubled our thread and gave them a bit more "stiffness" within the fabric of the medallion itself.

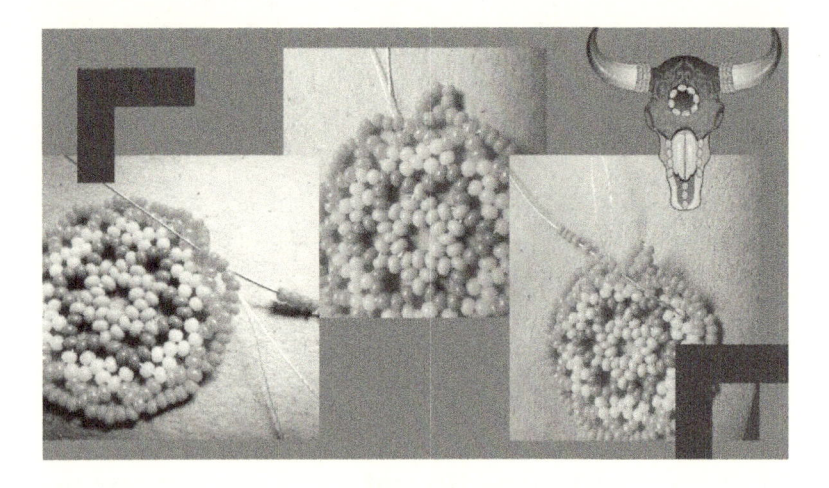

I'm going to heavily rely on our illustrations here to explain this particular spot of beading.

In the bottom left, you can see we begin by coming out of the middle of one of the fire red loops. Next, you will thread on five more red beads. It's good to use the same outlining color to finish your piece with this extra "topper."

Go back, as shown, and into the first red bead on your loop and also the middle orange, and come out of the first red beside that orange one. Look at your middle illustration to guide you. It seems complicated, but I swear it's not!

You will come out of the one red bead as in the middle picture, thread on five more red beads, and go backward back into the same two beads you just came out of—the last red bead on your loop and the middle orange one for a second time. Check out the bottom right picture to really get it right. If you don't understand the written instructions, simply thread on and through your edging to attach two loops of beads above the beadwork as shown.

What we are doing is adding two small loops of beads at the top. We want them to match and be centered, so our earring hangs well. Now we are going to attach the two loops with one bridging them at the top. This is the loop of beads our earring will use to become attached to the *finding*.

Tip #60 - Use the same color for your earring "toppers" as the edging color for a consistent look.

If there is no definitive edge color, pay attention when choosing your "topper" color for the best aesthetic advantage you can.

In the left image, you can see where we eventually came out after threading our second loop on the top of your medallion. First, thread your way up through the second bead in the loop and thread on five more red beads. Then, go down into the other loop at the top of the last two beads, as shown on the left.

I hope you can see this well.

Your ending "topper" will look like the image on the right as you follow my directions. If yours doesn't exactly match, I will leave you to decide what you would like to do about it. It's easy to pull the thread back out if you want to start over, but other combinations of beads can also work for your "topper." But a single loop of beads like our Brick Stitch earrings will not work well with these circular medallions.

I give this as an easy example. It's great practice to weave through your beadwork. And with these earrings, I simply thread the needle all the way down one side until I am at the bottom where I want to add dangles. Because my thread is already doubled, dangles can go on without a new piece of thread. I do tie-off with a knot before beginning my dangles. Yes, wink, wink, you know it, hide your knot into a bead, "pop," and get ready for dangles.

We will attach dangles to the two bottom loops directly below your "topper." I find the center orange bead on **the first loop to the left** of the direct-bottom-center. Then go into the first red bead beside the orange center bead to begin. After you begin to get experience adding dangles, you can put them wherever and however long you like. I hope my example will make this helpful.

So, as my thread comes out of the first red bead on a bottom loop, I string on my beads for a dangle. Next, I thread on three fire red, three orange, three yellow, three green, three white (I added a pop of white not in our medallion), and then 20 turquoise beads. Then I add to these three white, three green, three yellow, three orange, and finally three fire red to complete threading on one dangle's worth of beads. Can you see the pattern? It's simply a mirror of the other side of the dangle as we loop it into the earring edge.

Why so complicated? Oh, well, look at the finished product on the top right. Isn't it worth the extra complications? You will come to love the beautiful details of beadwork as you progress. I'm hardly scratching the surface of its intricacy. That's why it's such an art form in and of itself.

And now we **skip** a bead and slide our needle, with thread full of beads counted out for your dangle, into the next one on the loop. One dangle is attached. Look at the top left image. Do that. Repeat this same set of beads and attach the same way around the bottom red loops.

You will put on two dangles this way, skipping a red bead between as you attach them until you get to the very center, where you will do the same thing. Here you will skip the very center middle orange bead. It feels like a bead you should go into, maybe, but don't. Instead, attach your dangle on either side of it in the red beads beside the center orange one.

Continue threading your beads on, attaching the dangles by skipping a red bead on the other side. You will end up with five dangles altogether. Look at the upper right illustration and see how you did.

Is this confusing yet? Look at the diagram, go slowly, and enjoy the riddle as you unravel it.

Yours will look just as good as the one on the top right. I have no doubt!

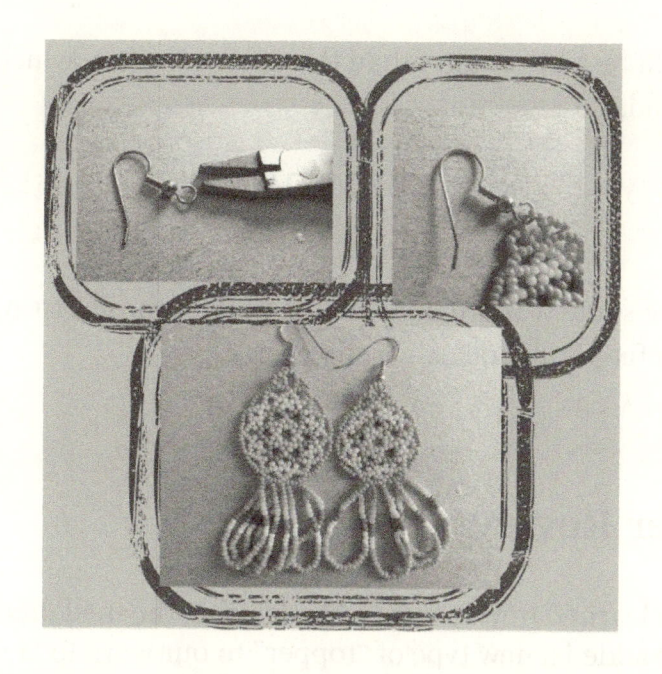

Now we get to do something really easy! I've included yet another type of earring *finding*.

Use your pliers as in the upper left image. Open the ring at the top of the wire hook. I am showing it opened by your pliers. When you get the hooks, they are a closed circle there.

Slide your "topper" beadwork into the loop as in the top right image.

Now simply squeeze the ring shut like it was before you opened it with your pliers.

Your earrings are ready to wear – that is – unless you made them different as I did! Look again at the center image, and you have two examples of the same earring. You weave them exactly alike, but simply start with ten beads in your center loop for the one on the right. It will be a bit smaller than the one on the left, which began with 12 beads.

Either way, your "FIRE COLOR MEDALLIONS" will be a hit. Well done.

Now I have some work to do to match both of these earrings. We ALL get to fix our mistakes—even experts.

Chapter Review

- We learned how to weave beads using the medallion stitch.
- We added a new type of "topper" to our work to facilitate our *findings*.
- We learned how to finish our medallion earrings with dangles and attach earring *findings*.

Chapter 7: Going Crazy with the Peyote Stitch

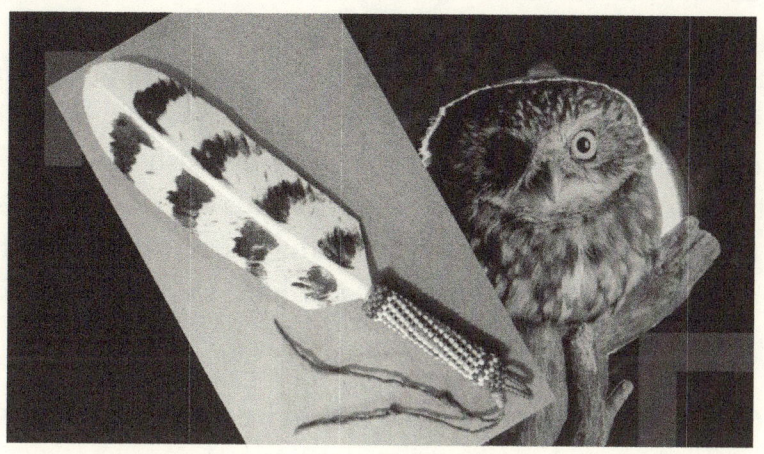

Peyote Owl Feather

Peyote is a naturally found drug some Native Americans have used through the years that could bring about weird and crazy hallucinations and dreams, and so forth. But, the name of the stitch here is used because doing this stitch can make you feel crazy by the time you're done! It's used as a joke; there's no peyote actually involved.

I've chosen an owl feather to bead around for our demonstration project. Owl feathers are illegal to even own, like many feathers. Native Americans are the only people deemed legal to use feathers and various animal parts in their regalia and ceremonial items. But this one is simply painted like an owl feather and purchased online, so no worries.

With the Peyote Stitch, you can bead around things or use it for flat projects as well. A traditional application back in the day was to bead around cigarette lighters. Key chain fobs are also a big hit with this stitch. A more intense project would be a full medicine pouch or other larger types of projects.

I've used it to "hold" on rabbit fur around a drum stick, beaded a small piece around a pipe, and even added a few inches of decoration around a small flashlight. It's a great stitch for including a spot of color to normal everyday things. However, you might not want to use it on something that's going to be washed a lot or will be likely to rub or bump against anything. Beads are made of glass and prone to break in some scenarios. Washing beadwork wears the string and other materials out, and your hard work in the beading will come unraveled.

Tip #61 - Peyote Stitch is called this because its intensely locking pattern takes concentration and time.

There are no shortcuts that will get you to the end faster. It's a bead-by-bead stitch like many others in Native American beadwork. (I'm not so sure why this one, in particular, is considered difficult.)

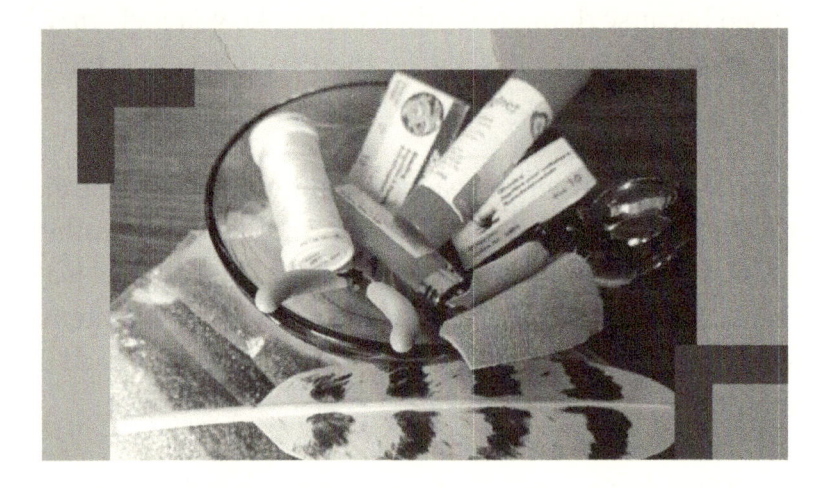

These are the supplies needed for your ornamental feather or other items you might be beading around.

Tip #62 - A common wooden kitchen spoon used for cooking is a great platform to bead around to make a key fob.

Just don't glue your leather to the handle so you can take it off when done!

I have two kinds of needles included here. One is a size 10 leather needle, and the other is a regular size 12 beading needle. You can use any color bead or layered combination you like as we go along. I did not include a pattern from peyote bead pattern paper, but once you practice this stitch, you will be able to experiment with a peyote pattern. I think you will be able to follow it very easily. Just remember that the Peyote Stitch is going to make you crazy no matter what pattern you use! That's why we love it. We can brag about that when we finish.

Here, you can see how a small piece of leather can be useful in beading projects. We only need a piece about two inches wide and however long you want your beadwork to become. I used no more than three inches long. I did leave the extra leather attached to my work and used the excess to create leather thongs hanging down, but it isn't necessary. I simply want to show you the many ways leather can be utilized in your work.

Tip #63 - You can use a beading needle to go through leather instead of a leather needle. However, beading needles are sold in long and short, and the short will work better.

Long beading needles bend more and break easily when used through the leather. Short needles are only about 1 ½ inches long and much more sturdy.

If you don't have a feather, use my expert tip about the cooking spoon and simply wrap your leather around this. Don't glue it to the handle; just wrap the leather around it and glue it to the leather only. At the end of our project, you will cut a leather thong, or use a piece of small cord, to fold in half and insert it into the space the spoon holder was using inside your leather and beadwork. (I will add directions for you as we go.)

This illustration above shows you the head of a leather needle; it typically has been cut with three sides at the point. The size 10 leather needle just barely goes through a size 12 bead, but probably only once. We will switch out our needles for beading as soon as the leather stitching is done.

Now we can begin!

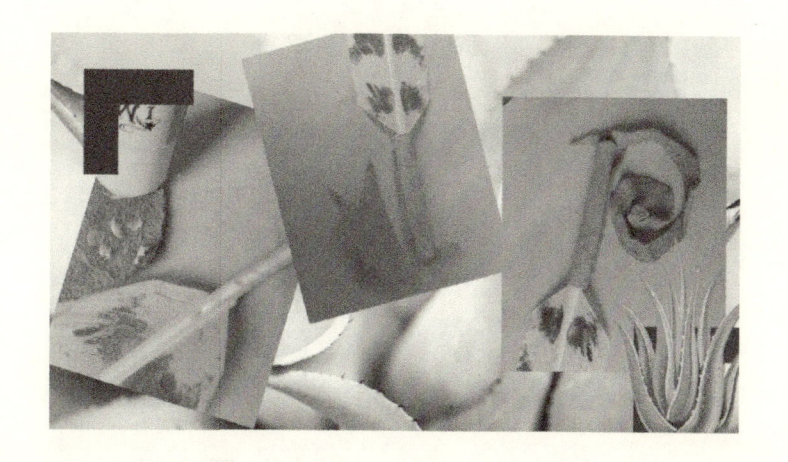

Cut your leather to the length of your feather stem as in the middle image. Take your plain old craft glue stick and rub some along one edge. I also applied the same glue to the stem of the feather. I like to leave a lot of it as shown because the leather will soak it up, and it doesn't show when dry on this.

Place your feather stem at the edge of the leather and roll inward, pressing the leather against the feather stem. I put enough glue along the edge, about an inch, to stick to the leather as it rolls around the feather stem. You can make this leather as thick as you like – simply roll it another time around.

I used my scissors and cut the piece left attached, as shown in your upper right image. You don't have to cut it until the end, actually. It got in my way while beading because of the strip hanging down. So, do it now or at the end of your work. Either way, you will have a nice piece of leather attached to use to tie onto something or for decoration.

I love how soft and natural leather is. The edges never fray, so you don't have to stitch extra for your projects.

Take an arm's length of thread and double it. Thread on your leather needle and make a knot with the ends together. Cut the ends and burn them up to the knot. We will insert that needle under the leather as in the upper left image. This will hide our knot for us.

Pull your thread through, and wrap the leather at the end of your feather stem or onto your spoon handle tightly. We want secure stitching to stabilize the leather base of our beadwork. The middle image shows you how we wrapped the leather tightly, then tied our thread to itself. This knot and thread will not show after the beadwork is on.

Begin stitching through your leather all the way up, as in the upper right image. Pull the leather as you go to slightly stretch it tightly. Leather has a lot of supple give as needed, unlike regular cloth.

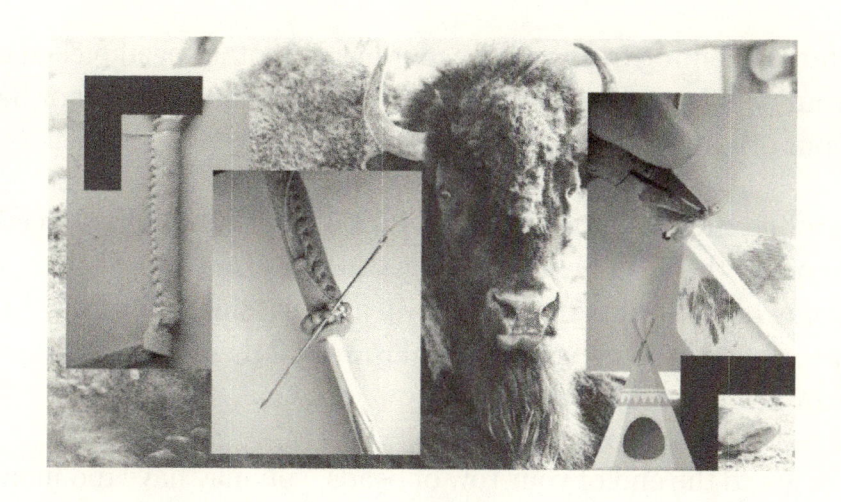

We will wrap the thread around the top as well as we did the bottom. Wrap tightly! Now it should look mostly like the upper left image. Pull tightly, make your knot, and cut and burn the ends.

As we begin our beadwork part, we take a double length of thread, an arm's length, and thread on your beading needle now. Pull your thread through the leather and tie it to the thread you left at the top. I begin at the top where the feather is because I can always cut the bottom as I go if needed.

Now we will thread on our first color of beads. With peyote, it's a guess at how many we need. Because the beads interlock, we only need beads for our first row about 2/3 of the way around our stem. We tie our thread off, so it doesn't come undone as we begin beading.

There are a lot of knots in our beginning steps for this project. Aren't you glad we don't have to hide them all?

Don't cut your thread after tying your first row onto the stem. Simply go through the first bead and cinch it down to the knot. Here is your anchor bead. In the middle picture above, you will see the thread coming from your anchor bead, another bead picked up on your needle and going into the next bead beside the anchor bead on your original first row.

Go around the whole row like this. Pick up a bead with your needle, and go into the bead next to the one you just came out of—no skipping beads in this stitch. You will attach a single bead in between each bead on your original row. Pull them towards your anchor bead as you go.

As we get to the end of your row of beads, you may have too many! This is always where your guesswork gets resolved. We want our bead rows tight, so don't add any more than what comfortably fits around your stem. In fact, look at the upper right illustration. However, many beads we have extra, we will cut out of our first row.

Cut your beads with your pliers. Then, simply grip the bead between the pliers and apply pressure. It's not easy, so don't give up. If you can't bust your bead, simply readjust your grip on it, and try a slightly different spot on the bead as you squeeze.

Tip #64 - Close your eyes and make sure no one is nearby when cutting out beads.

The glass shards can spray as the bead disintegrates.

The beads will pop loudly as they bust and may cut your thread. If you cut them from the side, it's a bit more difficult, but they are less likely to cut your beadwork thread. I will show you how I cut them from the side in the upper right picture.

I had to cut out two beads, so my beadwork was tight. Even so, I found it not to be as tight as I liked, and I will demonstrate how to reduce your row count a little further down. You may need this technique if beading around something that gradually gets larger or smaller anyway.

So, after the extra beads are cut out, you are back at the anchor bead you began with in the first row. Go through your anchor bead **again**, drop your needle down to the next row of beads and go through the very first one you attached to the anchor bead. Remember, your knot is right there if you've forgotten. And if you pick the wrong bead, we can still go forward, but you may have some strong showing.

Tip #65 - If there is string showing in your peyote beadwork, you probably skipped a bead somewhere.

You can go back and fix it as soon as you see it, or continue and simply cut the thread showing and burn the ends to make it disappear after your work is finished. Once your tightly woven beads are in place, likely, they won't come undone. But, you can also add some string and go through the beads attached to the string showing before you cut and burn. Tie off the string, pull the knot into a bead beside the knot, and cut and burn. Your work will be secure and the troublesome mistake hidden.

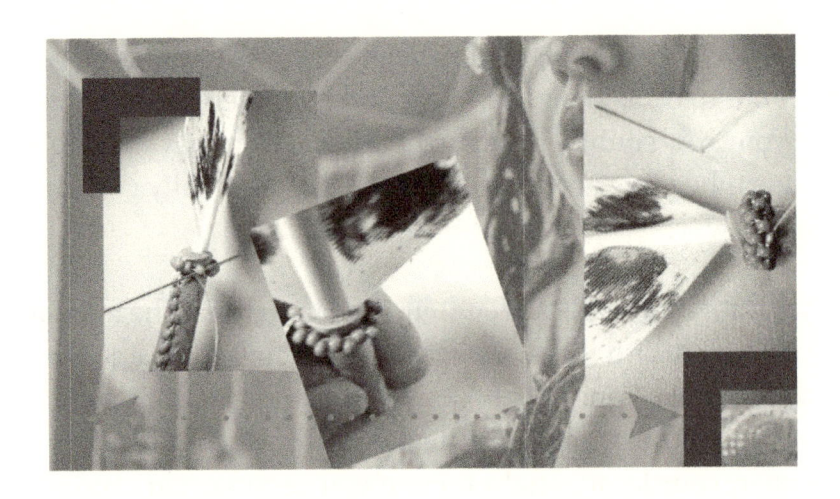

Here in the upper left image, you should be starting your next row like we just added the first. The middle image shows you what your beadwork will look like with the first row in place and the second-row beads in between added on. Your beads are going to most likely flare out to the side at this point, like this top view in the middle image. Don't worry; we will make it behave!

Now we will begin our third row with ease. I've used a darker bead with a gloss finish to add to the flat green. We come out of the second row of flat green, thread on a darker bead, and go into the next bead on the second row that's sticking out like in our image above. They are really easy to find. As we add a dark bead between each of the flat green ones, we will complete our third row. It looks like the upper right image.

Thread your needle out of a dark green one as shown in the upper right to begin our fourth row. Now you get the idea? It's a repetitive, one bead at a time, kind of stitch. You go round and round your stem with each row until you think you're done. Or, maybe, crazy?

Adding and Subtracting Beads in Peyote Stitch:

As you add rows, pull your thread tightly, but don't break your thread. Here's when you need that strong beading thread. Your beads will begin to lay flat around your feather stem or spoon handle as you pull them in. It's usually just the first two rows that give you issues with your beads trying to flare outwards.

But my beadwork is bulging just a bit, so I want to reduce one bead out, so it will lay flatter. If you care to do this, or if your stem gets narrower, you will need to learn to reduce your row of beads. It's one of the simpler "fixes" in beading.

As you begin to add your next row, mine is white beads, then just go through two beads on the row above it, like in the upper left image. Next, add a white bead as in the picture, and go through two beads instead of one to attach it. Usually, we attach a bead to every single bead in the row above it, but now we will go through two beads. Then carry on around as usual. Make sure to pull on your thread tightly as you go into the next bead so that it draws those two beads together. Keep your string tight as you go.

When you get around to the two beads pulled together, just treat them as if there's just one. Add one bead before them and one after them to look like the top middle image.

You have now reduced your row count by one bead without breaking anything out and causing a real headache.

I have two rows of original flat green, two rows of darker glazed green, and two rows now of white pearl-glazed beads. Finally, I add a row of brown opaque white-heart beads (the glass is clear but colored, and the center is powdered white).

Look at the lower center image. You can hardly tell those two beads are sitting together now, and our beadwork is much tighter and solidly hugging our leather. So it was a good fix.

If you want to add a bead, you simply string on two beads between the ones in the upper row instead of 1 bead as you would normally do. Then, as you go around, you treat the row like usual and put a bead between each bead when you start the next row, even between the doubled beads. This will add in an extra bead and open up your beadwork to enlarge your circle.

Tip #66 - The only time you can add or decrease extra beads into your row is when your pattern will allow it.

If you're going around with stripes like a barber pole or candy cane, it will mess up your pattern when adding or subtracting beads. And if you have a design on your peyote paper, make sure it won't interfere with it before you attempt to add or decrease beads.

I began the beadwork with three rows of green for a strong border color. Then I added two rows of dark green and two rows of white. You can sort of make out the pattern now. If you continue on like this, it will look like rows of V's or zigzags. That is a great colorful pattern by itself if you simply repeat it over and over, but I want to show you how to do stripes as well as zigzags.

As you can see, we used one row of brown, then began another of white. If you continue as I did, alternating between one row of brown and one of white, it creates stripes around your feather stem. They will gently curve around as you go without any effort to make them do that.

In the upper right image, you can see where I began using green beads in the place of the brown, but I kept the white consistent. I simply switched one color as I went. So now you have a nice effect, and we've kept the stripe running along.

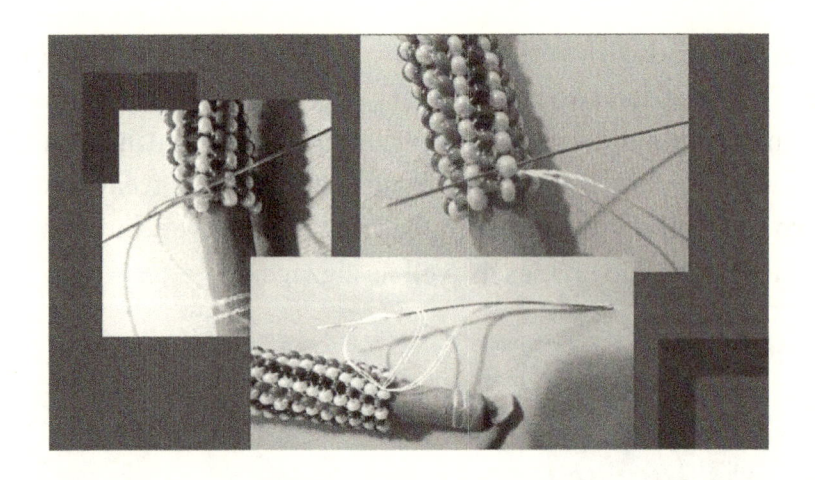

And now, I've done one-third in brown and white and switched to green and white for a middle third of the length. Then, I switch back for the last third, ending like I started, with brown and white stripes. You can make your pattern of stripes however you like. They can stay all brown and white, or whatever combination you prefer.

Tying in a new thread:

With this stitch, you will find yourself running out of thread a lot. Not to worry! We can easily tie in a thread and hide knots within this stitch. I'm even going to show you an easier way to begin your thread than attaching it to the beadwork. But, first, we will tie off your old thread.

In the upper left image, I pick up a thread within my beadwork with my old threaded needle. In the middle image, you can see how I wind the thread around my needle twice. As in the upper right image, this makes a very nice knot as you tighten it down.

Now you simply slide your needle through the bead beside the knot, pull in your knot into the bead, cut as closely to your beadwork as you can, and burn the ends. And we are ready to tie in a new long piece of thread.

Make a knot at the end of your new thread. Cut and burn it as close to the knot as possible. Pull it through the beads and go down to the bead where your beadwork left off. The knot will catch in the beads and stay within the beadwork itself. If you haven't practiced this yet in this book, then don't get frustrated. Take your time, and it will get easier as you go.

Continue now with one row of brown, alternating with one row of white. Your stripe will go on around, and you will bead the last third way down toward the bottom. Leave enough space to add another few rows for a bottom border to match the border we started with.

We will add two rows of dark green, two rows of white, two rows of lighter green, and then end with two rows of brown.

I have to say, my brown beads look a bit purple in the picture here. Purple would look pretty too. And you can use any colors you like.

So, when you get the bottom row of brown beads finished, what now? We want to be able to use this feather for something, right? Yes, of course, so we will add a small loop that you can use to attach to whatever you like. We can slide it on a hair barrette, tie it to a walking stick, or even use it on a drum for ornamentation—lots of possibilities.

In the upper left picture, I've threaded on 20 beads for the loop. In the middle image, I'm attaching them to a bead opposite of where your thread came out. Then, simply thread your needle back through the loop to make it very sturdy. Next, go into the opposite side of the bead you began the loop, as in the upper right image.

This will finish your beadwork. Did it make you "peyote crazy"? I hope not!

I've tied the leather strip hanging down into a knot at the base of the beadwork. This will add a bit of strength to your leather strand. Look at the upper left image.

Next, I cut the strip, slicing it up the middle as in the middle image. I wet the strips and finished by twisting them so that the effect is like the upper right image. You can have the raw strips hanging as they are, but I just like the look of the twisted leather.

Tip #67 - If you want to wet your leather to "work" it, use hot water.

The hot water softens it quicker and helps it twist better when punching a design into it.

And now you can see our finished peyote beaded feather in the upper right picture. I think you will really enjoy this finished project for years to come.

If using a spoon handle instead of a feather:

You will bead the same way we did, but now you will slide your beadwork off the spoon. Cut a piece of cord or leather strip about 20 to 25 inches long. Fold the cord, and slide the folded side into the center of your beadwork. Slide it all the way through until it comes out the top of your beadwork. Tie a knot as close against the top of the beadwork, leaving the folded loop end above it. Make sure the knot is large enough so that it can't be pulled back into your beadwork. Then pull down on the ends of the cords at the bottom end of your beadwork and tie another knot up against the bottom of your beadwork. Your beaded work should be caught between the knots with a loop at the top.

You will have extra strands of leather or cord hanging down below your bottom knot. You can wet them and twist them to look pretty if you like. The loop at the top will attach to a key ring or anything else you care to decorate.

Chapter Review:

- We began a Peyote Stitch project around a feather and learned how different colored beads make patterns within the stitch.
- We learned how to add in beads or take out beads if needed.
- We saw how to complete a project with the Peyote Stitch and finished it with a loop to hang onto something for decoration.
- We were given instructions on beginning and finishing the same Peyote Stitch around a spoon handle and using it for a key fob or decoration.

Chapter 8: Open Peyote Stitch

Open Peyote Medicine Pouch

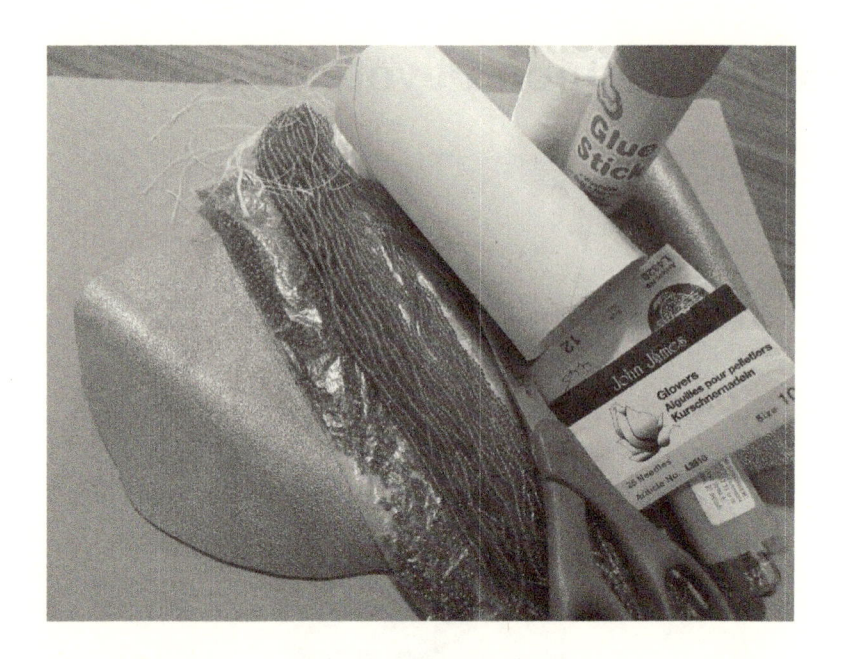

Now we go from Peyote Stitch to OPEN Peyote Stitch. Your supplies are shown above to create an Open Peyote medicine pouch. These particular medicine bags are very popular with Native American beaders. You will start with a piece of leather about five inches by four inches.

I didn't include it in the picture above, but we will use an awl for piercing holes into your leather. **Make sure you have an awl or a very good leather needle before you begin**. You can sew your pouch with a regular sewing needle or beading needle, but it will be a struggle.

I also will use a doubled thread for this whole project. Anytime I instruct you to add a thread, it should be doubled. I usually pull out a piece as long as my arm and double that to begin. You will be adding in a lot of thread for this Open Peyote Stitch.

You might have noticed the paper toilet roll. You can use a paper towel roll and cut it down if you like. But as weird as it may seem, the paper tubes work better than anything else I've found. I tried cutting a piece of PVC, and it was heavy and difficult. The edge of the plastic pipe kept catching my thread and tearing it. But, these paper tubes have proven successful. It's simply another example of the resourcefulness of the Native American culture. If you have someone looking at you weird as you bead, just call it *repurposing,* as is the new *popular* catchphrase. This is actually the authentic way I was shown to make these medicine bags by other Native American beaders. So, don't worry about it.

We will use leather needles and regular ones. I also have chosen a tri-cut bead that is just a shade lighter than your main aqua blue beads shown in the picture. You will notice the darker beads are the same colored aqua glass, but they have a dark center which you will see is going to look very purple in the application. These projects will teach you a lot about mixing beads and colors. Sometimes the results will surprise you. But mix them how YOU want them. I've seen many people pick bead colors and types for projects, and I've never seen an ugly combination. So be bold and be confident to choose whatever colors you like for your projects.

Leather is very available in packages of mixed scraps. I warned you about using leather scraps with a shiny or coated side other than raw leather. In this picture, I've chosen a scrap that is raw on one side with a golden wash on the opposite side. It will be more difficult to use, but my awl will prevail, and I wanted the color behind my beadwork to reflect the beads. Raw leather will look just as good if that is what you have. If you look at the finished bag at the beginning of this chapter, you will notice the leather is hardly even seen.

My scraps are never any certain shape. That's one reason they are cheap. This one is a bit curved, so I simply cut it to shape along a straight line I've drawn on the raw side, which will be inside the purse and not seen. Your leather piece should look like a rectangle when you're done.

I've cut it to fit just exactly around the paper tube and be about four inches high. Use the tube as your guide for your cut. Don't let your leather be loose around the tube. You want it to hug your tube, so it doesn't slide around as you bead.

We will take the top (simply pick one end or the other of your tube as the top) and sew the sides of the leather together around the tube using our leather needle or piercing holes with your awl.

Tie a knot to pull the ends together and begin stitching your leather along the length of your medicine bag. You can continue to stitch with your leather needle, but piercing holes along the side will help you tremendously if you are using a regular needle. So just begin this project with holes pierced by your awl.

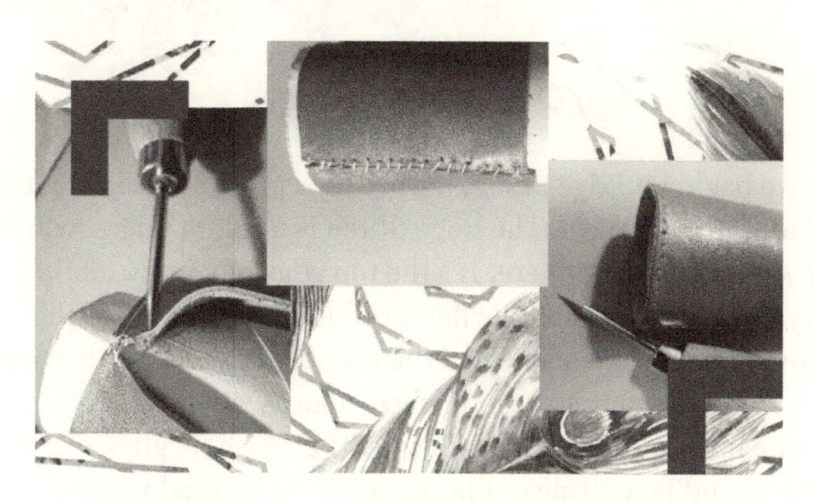

You can see from the middle image how the sewing progresses. When you get to the bottom of your side, knot the bottom edges together and cut and burn the ends. The knots are not really going to show much once we begin the beaded work over the top of the leather. Yes, you heard me. This is just your base for the beadwork.

When you're done with the side and it feels secure around your paper tube, we will punch holes around the top edge of your medicine bag. Insert each hole about ¼ of an inch all the way around the top edge. That's close, so try to make them evenly set in your leather. This is great practice with an awl! The more evenly spaced holes, the more even your beaded edging will be.

See the top right image of mine as I finished.

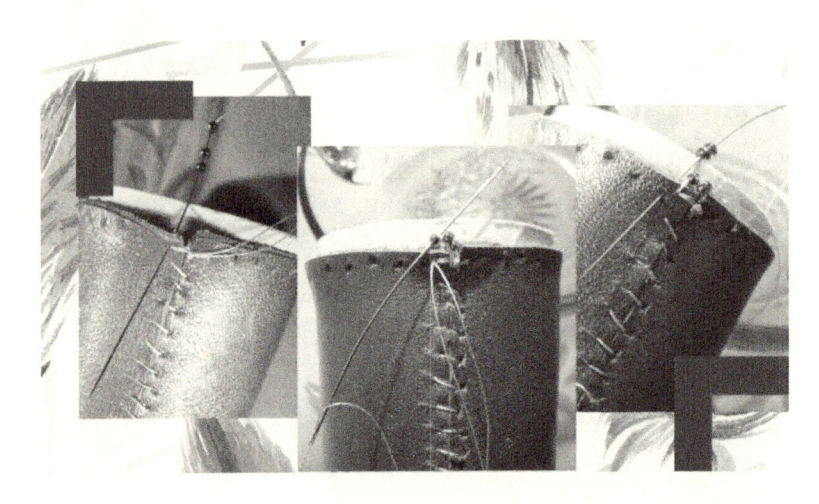

Here we begin an Edge Stitch. Surprise! Yep, we are learning two stitches for this project. The Edge Stitch is used for edges, which is what we are looking at here. It's the top edge of your work. In reality, I'm saving you all the hassle of doing it like we did the Peyote Stitch where we guessed the number of beads, yada yada... This will allow you to have a finished edge as you begin and continue into your new Open Peyote Stitch with no guesswork involved. And no cutting out beads which I personally hate.

This is my personal design as your expert bead guide, and you are the very first people to begin Open Peyote stitching in this way. I haven't even shared it with my beading friends. Wow, they might be mad now. So I will simply tell them Mr. Coyote was busy. He is always the trickster in Native American stories.

Edge Stitch:

We will begin at the top edge where your knot is still hanging out from sewing the leather. You have pierced holes about a ¼ inch all the way around. Tie your thread onto the knotted thread itself from sewing your leather. We will use it to anchor your thread. I'm using the darker beads to begin my Edge Stitch. Slide on three beads and go into the closest hole, as shown above in the left image. Go in from the back to the outside. Now take your needle back through one bead only, and pull up, as in the middle image.

You will see the first three beads attached in the upper right image. They sit a little crooked, but that will resolve itself at the end.

Tip #68 - Taking the time to use an Edge Stitch will always finish your beadwork with style.

The Edge Stitch has several applications, but finishing your work is its main attraction.

You will now repeat the same thing; however, you will only pick up two beads each time from here on out. So pick up two beads, go through the next hole, and come up through the last bead. You can see that your thread comes up out of a bead and begins to make a pointed edge as it goes back into the next set of beads. You can use five beads and do the exact same stitch, but it will be more open and tend to catch on things, so I recommend only using the three bead sets at a time for finishing your work. You can experiment with edging on your new projects as you progress.

Look closely at the images. Compare them to your work. The edging should look like the middle bottom image for the most part. Now you can see how the spacing of the holes is important. If you're using a needle, you simply go through the leather right next to the last one as if there was a hole there.

You can see how we end this Edge Stitch in the top right image. As you come to the first set you beaded, just pick up one bead instead of two. You've been using only two the whole way around, but for the last one, use only one bead. Go into the very first bead you put on from the top going downward, and tuck your needle to the back to come into the front of its hole, back to front. This will pull that first bead up to where it's in line with the rest.

Did that confuse you? I wouldn't be surprised. Go through the bead as shown in the upper right image. Then go behind it and push your needle through the hole it's attached to from the back to the front. I don't know how to explain it any better. Thank goodness for pictures.

Now, I would tie off my thread, but if you have a lot left, don't bother cutting it. We will continue now into the Open Peyote Stitch. Your simple edging is completed.

Slide your needle out of the top of the first three beads, as in the upper left image. Next, thread on five beads and only go through the next *top bead*. That's also shown in the top left image.

Do this all the way around. Pick up five beads every time and go into the next top bead in your Edge Stitch. It's going to look crowded and kind of lumpy. Keep your thread pulled tight each time you go into a new bead. It will look like the bottom middle image. If your added loops get too tight to put into the next center bead of your edging, then skip that one and jump to the next center bead. This will adjust your beadwork to the right amount of loops for you. This is why doing it this way keeps you from having to cut out beads. I only had to skip the very last set of five as it got so tight the beads couldn't fit in between the last set of five. And that's perfectly fine. If you don't get it, keep trying!

As we go, you'll see if you have too many loops, and you can back out the beadwork if necessary. Backing out is just cutting off your needle and pulling the thread backward to the point you need to restart.

These loops feel like they are going all over the place, don't they? Just wait.

As you come all the way around the edge, you will end up where you began. Go up into the middle bead of the first row of five beads to start the next section. Your needle will be coming out of the middle bead only of the first set of five. We are now going to make these beads behave.

Tip #69 - Much of Native American Beading is repetition.

Simple things combine within these stitches to form complex patterns. Much of nature is like that too. We get many patterns from things like pine cones interlocking tabs to feathers layering under a bird's chest. Repetition is a soothing and natural occurrence.

Your first beaded layer added to your Edge Stitch is going to feel a bit out of control. But now, we will help it to stabilize.

Simply go around this layer, adding one single bead between each middle bead of each loop. I've begun using the lighter-colored aqua beads now. As you can see in the images, we are only working the tip bead of the loop of five. Go into the tip, middle bead, thread on one lighter colored bead, and go into the next set *middle* bead. Look at the images. Can you see in the middle image where your beadwork was standing up and how the one bead between the loops is pulling it down into place? Yes, it's a miracle, I know. It's starting to behave itself. We can't let Mr. Coyote run wild.

The beaded layer is now beginning to hug your paper and leather tube. As you go, keep your thread pulled tight. At the end, in the upper right image, you will pull your thread tightly but not too tight to break it. Your beaded layer will lay mostly flat now against the tube. You can see some small spaces of thread left between, but it's good. This means your beads will continue to hug the cardboard tube.

Tie off your thread before beginning the next layers. You don't have to cut your thread if you have a lot left. Simply tie a knot and pull the knot into a bead close by and get ready to proceed. The tightness you've achieved needs to be anchored into place so you can now bead a bit more effortlessly, advancing your Open Peyote stitching. It's about to get very beautiful now!

Add your thread now, or continue after tying off your knot. Remember: the shortcut to adding thread within a weave is to make a knot at the end of your thread, cut and burn the ends, and simply pull it into the beadwork through the beads until it catches. The ongoing weave keeps the added knot from working loose. The beadwork helps you sometimes.

However, if you added thread or simply tied your knot, bring your needle out of one of the light blue beads to begin a new row, as in the left image. Thread on five light aqua beads; skip the next blue bead to go into the next one. Also shown in the left image.

Go all the way around your tube, making your new row of light aqua beads in sets of five. Then, pick up **every other** aqua bead to connect your new row. It will look like the middle image when you're done. You can see the lighter bead we skip between each loop of five beads.

In the bottom right, you can see where you slide your needle down into the row you just finished, to the middle bead of that loop of five. Come out the middle bead to begin your new row. You will only pick up the middle bead on each loop as you go around adding your new row. Slide on five beads, go into the middle bead of the loop, and slide on five more beads; repeat around.

I made three rows of light aqua beads. Simply continue around and around until you feel the Open Peyote Stitch trying to make you crazy. The upper right image shows you the ongoing rows happening as you add one and then another.

It will yield a very beautiful open, lace-like weave for the outside of your leather bag.

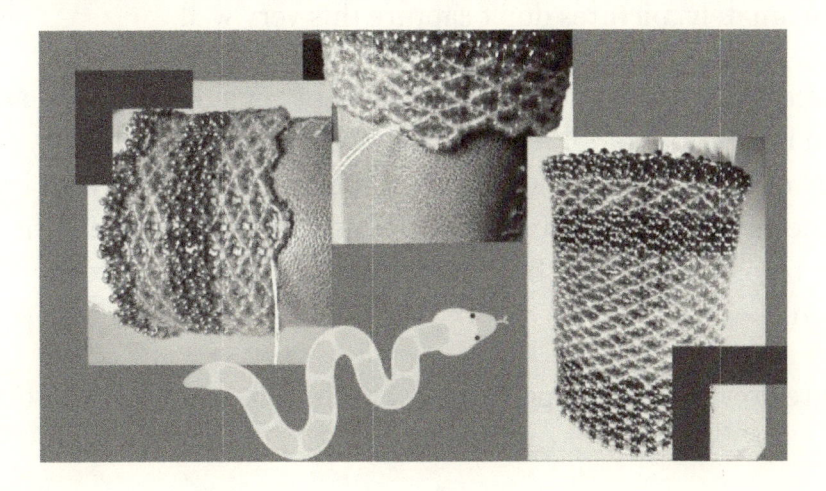

As you can see in the right and left images, I sewed on three layers of five aqua beaded loops, then switched to the darker blue beads. Finally, I sewed five rows of those the same as the aqua beads.

Now you can also see how I switched back to the aqua beads for six rows of plain aqua beads. We will be making these Open Peyote rows all the way down your tube, so they completely cover your leather medicine bag. And I want to add some sparkle and interest to our plain rows.

I have now included a tri-cut bead as the middle bead of each loop of five that I add. So, slide on two aqua beads, one aqua tri-cut, and two more aqua for each loop. Then, make the rest of your rows like this. You won't believe the sparkle that happens from adding these in.

In the bottom right image, you can see the tri-cuts a little more clearly mixed in the darker blue rows. Look up into the rows above that, and you can see them within the aqua as well. You will definitely be able to see them in your beadwork as you go. Unfortunately, pictures don't capture this very well.

I sewed five rows of plain aqua, six rows of aqua with tri-cuts, and seven rows of darker blue with tri-cuts. As you can see, the beadwork has reached the bottom of the leather bag. Tie your knot, cut the ends, and pull it into a bead. I usually thread up into the work before cutting and burning the end if I have some extra thread.

We are done with our Open Peyote Stitch! But, not done with the bag...

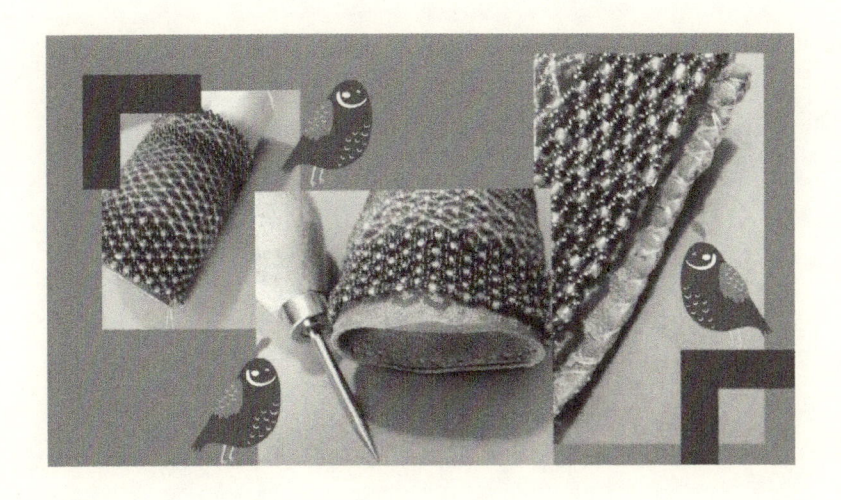

Time to drag out your awl again!

You will pull back the beadwork by sort of scrunching it up the tube. Just far enough to poke your holes into the leather all the way around the bottom of your leather. Slide the leather off the tube as shown in the middle image.

Now you can flatten the leather with the original seam to one side, not in the middle. Next, stitch the bottom together, as shown in the image on the right. I go all the way down one side through the holes, then cross stitch over the same way back. It will be fairly secure that way.

Tip #70 - Weaving your needle through your beadwork when adding thread helps your knot to be more secure.

It is one more way to add security to your work so your work will not come undone if your knot fails for one reason or another while wearing or using the beaded item.

Now we will pull our beadwork back down to the bottom and sew it together, as shown above. Again, I simply capture two of the tri-cuts to pull them together, as in the upper left image, then go back through them, as in the middle image.

Slide your needle through your beadwork to come up between the next tri-cut beads. Repeat all the way down the bottom, using your beadwork in between to move your needle through so your thread isn't showing as you go.

And this is what your finished bag will look like. It is really a beautiful bag. As you can see, each set of tri-cuts along the bottom lets us have a great place to hang our dangles.

This bag gives you a lot of practice with going through beads multiple times. We will be going through those same tri-cuts to attach our dangles. If they won't let you go through them, you can use a bead along the bottom nearby to attach it to. No one will notice.

Tip #71 - If you are going through beads more than once, your needle may give you trouble going through a stubborn bead. Simply push the tip through the bead, grab the tip of your needle with your pliers, and pull gently.

If it absolutely refuses to slide through, simply back it out and try to insert your needle in again to the edge of the hole in the bead, or slightly at an angle. Sometimes the thread will give way, so you can succeed with a little patience. However, if you pull too hard with your pliers, you may risk the bead breaking.

Start from one end of the bottom of your bag. Tie on your thread, come through your beads, and go out of the first tri-cut we used to sew our bottom beadwork together. Look at the left image. I strung a lot of beads onto my thread and looped it back up through the tri-cut next to the one I started with. You can make your dangles however you like, in whatever pattern you like, and however long. You can also add more dangles as you like to your purse.

However, I will add my pattern to help if you need it. I have made *graduating* dangles. They become longer or shorter as you go, to give a V shape to the end product. If you want your dangle even all the way across, then don't use graduating dangles. Simply use the same set of beads for each dangle.

Look at the upper left image to see how you weave your needle through the beadwork to come to the next dangle. This is not difficult, and otherwise, you have to tie on each dangle which is very tedious.

Here is the way I put on beads to make my dangles:

1)- 3 dark blue, 1 aqua, 1 aqua tri-cut, 1 aqua, 13 dark blue, 1 larger white, 5 aqua, 1 aqua tri-cut, 5 aqua, 1 aqua tri-cut, 5 aqua, 1 larger white, 13 dark blue, 1 aqua, 1 aqua tri-cut, 1 aqua, 3 dark blue.

This is simply the first dangle. I will only increase the dark blue beads on each one until we get to the middle dangle; then, I will go back and decrease the way I put them on. But in case it's too difficult, remember to look at our first image in this chapter, which will show you the dangles.

I will continue the list of bead counts for all nine dangles that I added:

2)-5 dark blue, 1 aqua, 1 aqua tri-cut, 1 aqua, 15 dark blue, 1 larger white, 5 aqua, 1 aqua tri-cut, 5 aqua, 1 aqua tri-cut, 5 aqua, 1 larger white, 15 dark blue, 1 aqua, 1 aqua tri-cut, 1 aqua, 5 dark blue.

3)-7 dark blue, 1 aqua, 1 aqua tri-cut, 1 aqua, 17 dark blue, 1 larger white, 5 aqua, 1 aqua tri-cut, 5 aqua, 1 aqua tri-cut, 5 aqua, 1 larger white, 17 dark blue, 1 aqua, 1 aqua tri-cut, 1 aqua, 7 dark blue.

4)-9 dark blue, 1 aqua, 1 aqua tri-cut, 1 aqua, 19 dark blue, 1 larger white, 5 aqua, 1 aqua tri-cut, 5 aqua, 1 aqua tri-cut, 5 aqua, 1 larger white, 19 dark blue, 1 aqua, 1 aqua tri-cut, 1 aqua, 9 dark blue.

5) (Middle dangle)-11 dark blue, 1 aqua, 1 aqua tri-cut, 1 aqua, 21 dark blue, 1 larger white, 5 aqua, 1 aqua tri-cut, 5 aqua, 1 aqua tri-cut, 5 aqua, 1 larger white, 21 dark blue, 1 aqua, 1 aqua tri-cut, 1 aqua, 11 dark blue.

6)-9 dark blue, 1 aqua, 1 aqua tri-cut, 1 aqua, 19 dark blue, 1 larger white, 5 aqua, 1 aqua tri-cut, 5 aqua, 1aqua tri-cut, 5 aqua, 1 larger white, 19 dark blue, 1 aqua, 1 aqua tri-cut, 1 aqua, 9 dark blue.

7)-7 dark blue, 1 aqua, 1 aqua tri-cut, 1 aqua, 17 dark blue, 1 larger white, 5 aqua, 1 aqua tri-cut, 5 aqua, 1 aqua tri-cut, 5 aqua, 1 larger white, 17 dark blue, 1 aqua, 1 aqua tri-cut, 1 aqua, 7 dark blue.

8)-5 dark blue, 1 aqua, 1 aqua tri-cut, 1 aqua, 15 dark blue, 1 larger white, 5 aqua, 1 aqua tri-cut, 5 aqua, 1 aqua tri-cut, 5 aqua, 1 larger white, 15 dark blue, 1 aqua, 1 aqua tri-cut, 1 aqua, 5 dark blue.

9)-3 dark blue, 1 aqua, 1 aqua tri-cut, 1 aqua, 13 dark blue, 1 larger white, 5 aqua, 1 aqua tri-cut, 5 aqua, 1 aqua tri-cut, 5 aqua, 1 larger white, 13 dark blue, 1 aqua, 1 aqua tri-cut, 1 aqua, 3 dark blue.

Could you follow all of that? I'm not sure I could. But I am expecting everyone to do a great job on your dangles; however they come out.

We need to make a loop of beads at the top edge of your bag so that we can have a clasp to close your purse. I have devised a secondary catch that will ensure your bag doesn't come open.

Look at the right image above and find a spot near the center of your top edge. Tie in a new piece of thread and hide your knot after cutting and burning. We will thread on 40 beads and go back into a bead next to the one you began with. Thread back into your 40 beads now, and go back to the first bead you started this. Go back into it, thread your needle up into your beadwork and, tie it off, cut, burn, hide your knot.

Basically, you will add 40 beads on as a loop, go back through them so they are doubly secure, and tie them into your beadwork. The image shows you the end result.

You will have a loop of beads hanging from the top edge of your bag. Remember, the finishing work is rather tedious. Dangles are the most tedious, in my opinion. But we have a few more steps until we are done. Just a little more patience!

Now we begin on the front of your bag. It should be the opposite side from the loop of beads you just added. As you can see in the top left image, we will tie in a thread, as shown above, and attach three larger white beads. Tie a knot behind them to secure them in one spot of the purse. Then go out the middle bead and thread on ten aqua beads, one aqua tri-cut, and nine more aqua beads. Go back into the tri-cut as shown in the middle image. Add ten more aqua beads and tie them into the beadwork through your white beads, as in the top right image.

This will be part of the *catch* for your loop on the other side. It's actually simply a small dangle attached to your white beads.

Now we will pick a semi-precious bead–one that is big enough to slip through your dangle *catch* of aqua beads. Attach the semi-precious stone to your beadwork right below your three white beads. I chose an amethyst. It's a simple one-bead attachment.

To hold your purse together, look at the image on the right. I slide the aqua blue bead dangle through the dark loop and then bring it over and down to catch over the semi-precious stone. This acts as a double catch for your dark loop of beads.

Just pulling the aqua beads through the loop will catch it as well, but it can open when wearing your medicine bag with the movement of your body. If you slide it over the semi-precious stone as well, then it will be mostly secure.

As you look at your bag, I'm sure you're amazed you accomplished such an intricate piece of work. And you should be proud. These medicine bags are made a lot and are very popular among Native American beaders. This is not a beginner project, so cut yourself some slack if it was a bit difficult. Your skills have greatly advanced working through it.

But we have one more step. I take a double strand of thread for all projects requiring a strand of beads around the neck. You need it to be sturdy to hold up that Open Peyote work.

Add in a thread to the side of your bag at the top edge. Fasten it securely. You will have one very sturdy knot, or you can even knot it in two places before coming out a top bead on the edge.

Add on beads in whatever style and pattern you like for your necklace part. I made sure to add in a few white beads to finish tying them in with the rest of the purse. White always catches the eye and is great to separate your patterns as you go. I added about 40 aqua, then 60 darker blue, then 80 aqua; I separated the colors using the white beads. Then I continued backward for the other side. I continued with 80 aqua, 60 darker blue, then another 40 aqua.

Make your strand however you like, and it also depends on how many beads you have left in what colors. For example, I had a lot more aqua beads at the end of the project. So I used more of them for the necklace strand I attached.

Make sure to attach your thread to the other side of your bag as securely as you began your necklace part. And now your medicine pouch is finished. Great work! Hopefully, you aren't *peyote crazy*.

Chapter Review:

- Working with leather and an awl was used for this project.
- Beginning our work with the Edge Stitch was demonstrated.
- Open Peyote Stitch was used for the main body of this project.
- We learned how to finish this piece with *graduating* dangles, beaded catches, and adding a necklace strand of beads.

Chapter 9: Loom Beading

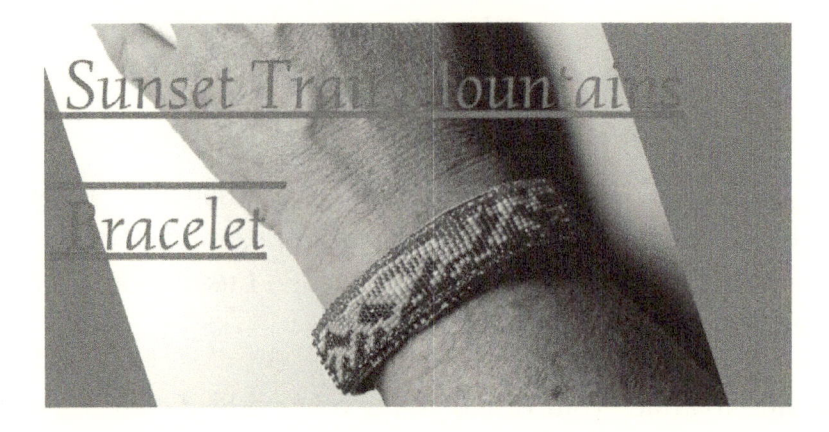

Do you love the mountains? I can almost feel the coolness of the evening from being high and free among the trees and wildlife that abound in mountain places. That is what inspires our next project with cool blues for the mountains and a dazzling sunset as we hurry down the trail to our campsite. We will construct this bracelet using a loom. It's my absolute favorite way to bead.

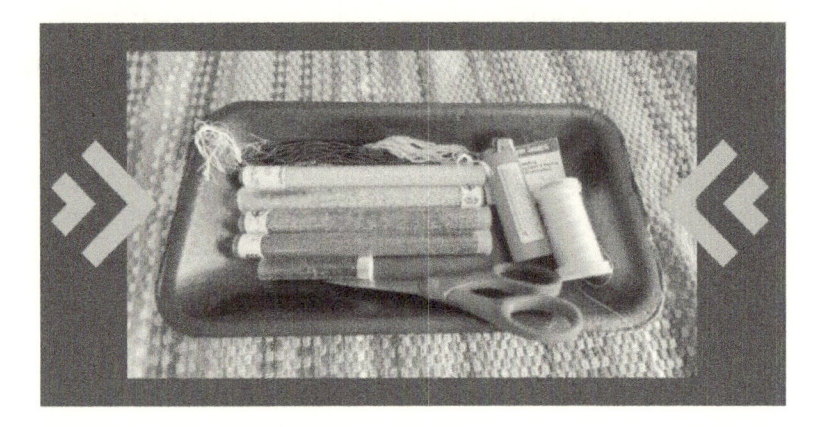

Above will be the necessary supplies for your bracelet, including the loom. I know. You can't see a loom in this picture. Well, there is one! Looms come in all shapes and sizes, and until you've done a bit of looming with beads, I suggest you try a typical supermarket meat tray.

The black foam tray above will serve us as a loom. It can be strung like any other loom for this small project and dips in the middle enough to allow your hand to move beneath the beads as you weave them onto the strings.

I've used small cardboard boxes many times, and the *Tandy Co* has a very popular beginner loom you can purchase online if you want to begin small. It's designed to introduce beading to children and interested craft enthusiasts. But we can start with no money out-of-pocket today.

The only thing you will need, not showing (oops!), is a strap of leather for the bracelet and a favorite bead or button for our smooth clasp.

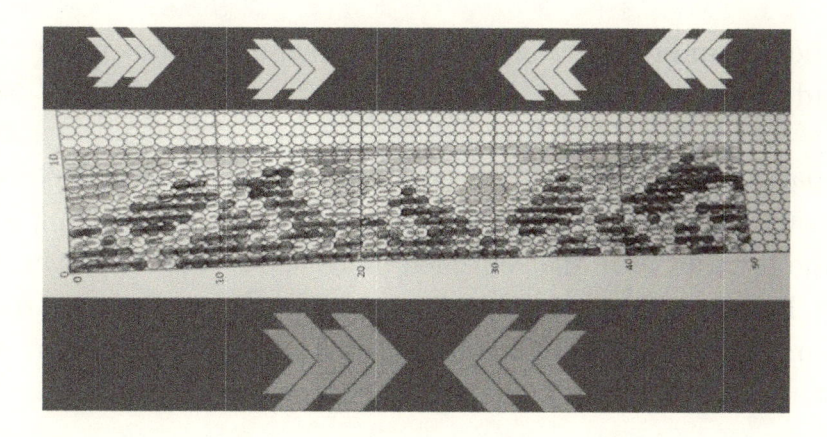

Here is your basic pattern created with loom beading paper. Be careful as you progress to watch for the peach and red bead colors. They tend to be difficult to discern from each other in my pattern. I used colored pencils, but you can always create your own with brighter colors for yourself. It might be great practice, hint, hint...

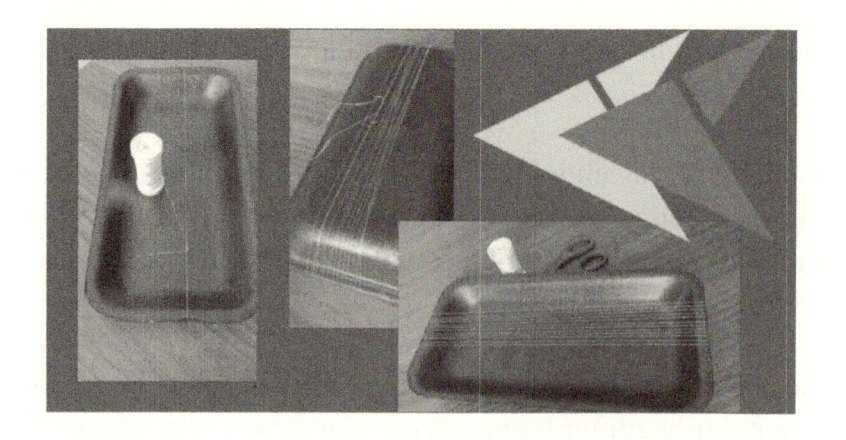

We begin our loom work by setting up our loom. This is not double threaded. You will wind your threads over and under and keep them pulled taut but not too tight. We don't want to cut into the foam tray too much.

Tip #72 - You always set up a loom with one more string as your rows in your bead pattern.

So, count your beads across in the pattern and wind one more thread to your loom.

Our pattern has 11 beads involved, so we will string 12 loom strings onto our foam tray. To do that, you will simply wind the string around the tray, as in the above left image, and tie the string in place. Remember, we want tension on all the threads, not just one or two. Think of a guitar and how you can press against the strings, and they give you resistance. That is what we need.

Tip #73 - Keep ALL threads on your loom taunt before you begin as you set up your loom.

If even one thread sags, you will have difficulty the whole way through your project, and your beadwork will not look even.

A 12-strand loom will be an easy start for learning this technique. After you make your knot, slide it around to the back of the loom as in the middle image. Then wind more strands around your tray until you count 12 loom strings on the front side of your tray. Keep your strand taut as you go, or you may end up with something that looks more like a bird's nest.

Tie off the last string in the back to the original knot to complete setting up your loom. As you make your knot, be sure not to let your strings go loose. Instead, pull on them as you lock down your knot.

Look at the middle image and the image on the right. This is basically how it should look. Not too difficult, but the first time may take a few more minutes as you learn to space the threads out just a touch. I usually wind them about a quarter of an inch apart, so they aren't tempted to cross over or tangle with the next thread.

Tip #74 - Waxing your loom threads will give them longevity and protect against the natural elements around you.

You can rub the wax over your loom threads before you begin, and here is another place you can use heavier thread as you like. However, it may show and interfere with your pattern if the thread is too heavy.

For your beading we are about to begin, use the regular weighted beading thread, and don't use double strands. This is one project where it can get in your way if you double your thread. The thread will be going in and out of your beads several times, and a double strand can get stuck as you try to weave.

I also used tri-cut beads to pop the darker places in the mountain. They take up the most room on your pattern, so they will give the most sparkle we want. I also looked at the light blue highlights over the mountains and realized white would make them look snow-topped.

As I analyzed my color choices, I probably would have used some brighter yellows too. But, all in all, the pattern is a nice one and sufficient for our learning needs. By the way, there are gobs of patterns available online to inspire you or buy to download.

I've always liked to make my own patterns. I like my designs to reflect something that brings me joy in life or represents a story or place I've lived. So many things have inspired me.

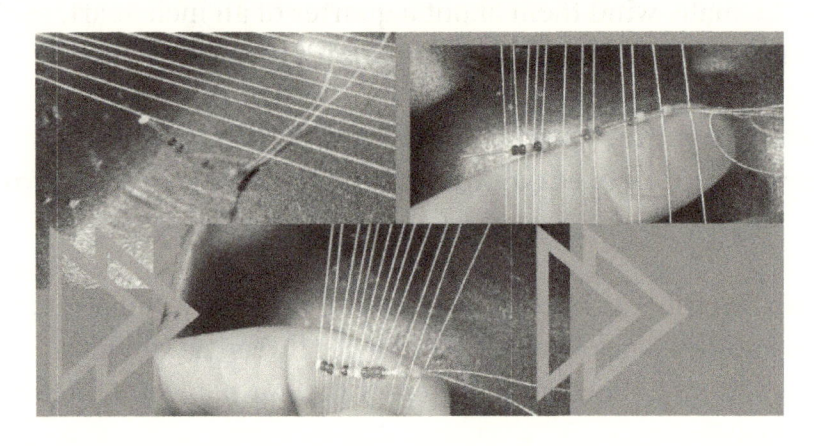

Now we tie on a thread to the outside thread of your loom. Start on either side. I usually begin from the left and go to the right. So I tie my thread on the outside left strand on the loom. Then I check my pattern and thread on the appropriate bead colors, following my pattern like the image below.

If you look above right, you can see our knot, and the beads will be led below your loom strands. Then you push them up through the spaces between your loom threads—one bead per space. The middle image above shows you how they will go.

I have to encourage you about now. You've set up a loom nice and taut, and the first line of beads is the most difficult. This one line will space your threads, so the rest are easier.

Hold them in place after you push them up while you slide your needle back through them, as in the upper right image. Slide over the top of the loom threads as you go back through the beads, or they can simply fall off. The thread below and one above your loom threads will hold them in place.

Now you've come back to the same place you began with one row of your pattern in place. Hooray!

Before going forward, stop, check our image above to make sure you counted the beads correctly and understand how to follow the pattern. Can you see the completed row? If so, paddle your canoe on down the river as we go to promising hunting grounds.

Tip #75 - Use a highlighter to mark your rows as you add them to the loom.

You can either mark all the way through your completed row or make a check along the side. If you simply use the checks, your pattern will still be able to be used again without difficulty. This may seem tedious at first glance, but it will save you a LOT of trouble by not having to remove a whole row if you make a mistake.

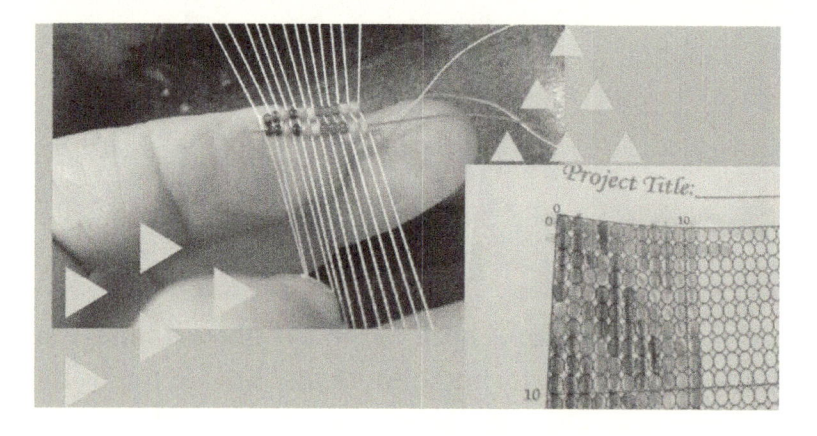

The first completed row of your pattern should be stabilizing your loom thread, so this next row seems to just *want* to slip into place. Careful to put only one bead in each slot.

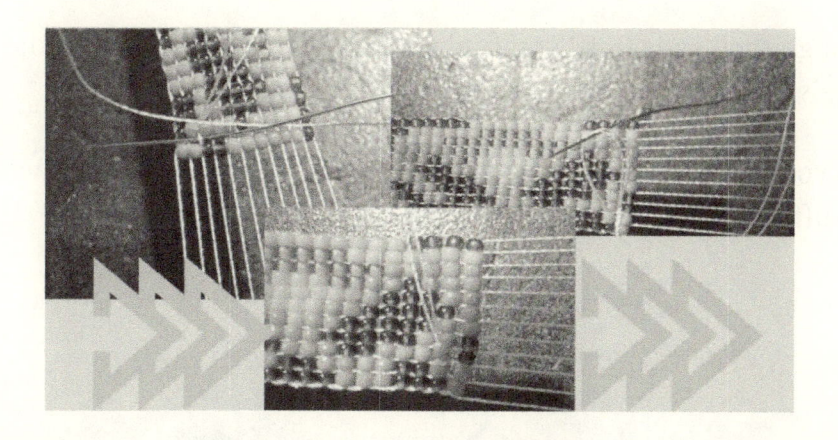

As you progress adding rows, you will probably run out of thread. So, we will finish a row of beads, tie a knot onto the first loom thread, and cut. Or, you can get back to the beginning of your row, slide your needle into a neighboring bead above, tie it off, pull it into the bead, and cut the ends. This will hide your knot better.

I only tie off onto the first thread of my loom to end my thread if I'm planning on using an Edge Stitch to finish my work. This is because as you add the Edge Stitch, it tends to hide knots along the side if they aren't hidden in the beadwork itself.

To add in more thread, you can tie a knot on the side if you are ending your project with an Edge Stitch. If you want to hide your knots, which is always a great general practice, look at the images above.

In the above left, I slide my needle under a loom thread of my choice near the spot I will be starting up again. Make a loop, go through it with your needle, pull it down onto the thread you picked up, and pull tight. Look at the upper right image.

In the middle image, we have simply *popped* that knot into a bead beside it and pulled through. Next, you will slide your needle through the beads until you find your starting point again on the side. Now you can proceed with your pattern.

Can you see why we DON'T double thread in looming? Yes, it would get difficult.

I also need to show you how to pull out a line of beads if you put the wrong ones on. It happens more than you might imagine. Above, you can see that I'm going to always pull the beads by loosening the thread on the opposite end and pulling that to take out the mistaken line. Once you loosen it with your needle, you can grab it and gently pull.

The needle will be trailing and slide through with your thread back through the beads if you want to do that, but it's easier just to take the needle off. Pull the thread out of the beads, slide off the wrong beads, and put your needle back on to start again.

Tip #76 - Be very careful when burning your loose threads as you use a loom.

If the loom threads burn, your work gets WAY complicated!

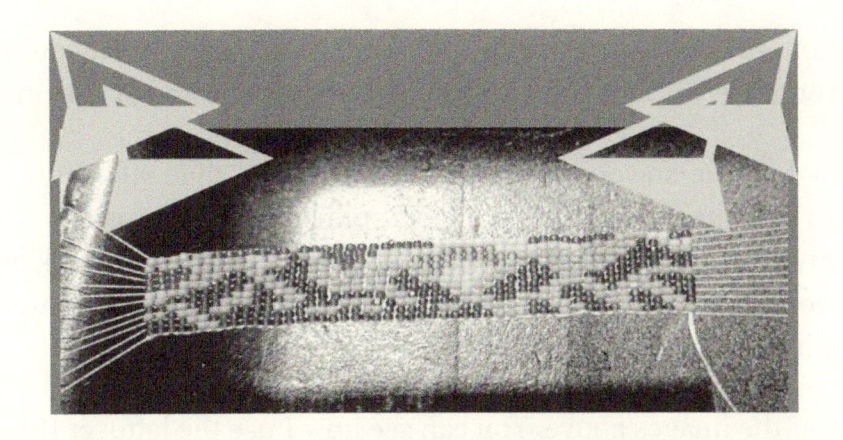

Here is what your loom work should basically look like when finished. Caution: DON'T CUT YOUR THREAD YET. The next step will use your leftover thread still attached.

The piece will become even more lovely as we add an edging at the end. Don't forget to plan for the edging color, your background colors, and other similar choices **before** you begin.

There are several ways to end your loom piece. Some people cut it from the loom and physically thread a needle on each strand hanging and weave them back into the beads, one strand at a time. I don't particularly recommend that process. When your beading is cut from the loom, it tends to be difficult to manage, and if you're not very careful, your beads can slide right off one end or the other.

If you don't finish your ends off, your beads will slide off. And you're very lucky you have an expert guide here. I know a very effective process to use. Not only does it secure your beadwork onto the loom threads, but it makes it possible to use as an anchor when finishing your work.

Look at the images above. You can see how I use the leftover thread at the end of my work to begin weaving in between the loom threads. I go one direction, then turn and go the opposite way, weaving between each thread. Slide each newly woven piece up against your beading as you go. It will look like the image in the middle. And when it's about three-quarters of an inch wide, tie it off on one side. Don't worry about the knot.

In the image above to the right, we take our glue stick and get a lot of sticky glue onto your woven thread base. This really secures your weave for our finished product. Let it sit overnight to dry if you like. But we can keep going if you don't want a break.

Tip #77 - Look closely at your loom work before cutting your loom.

Sometimes a mistake may be there, and you can rectify your work before it's absolutely too late.

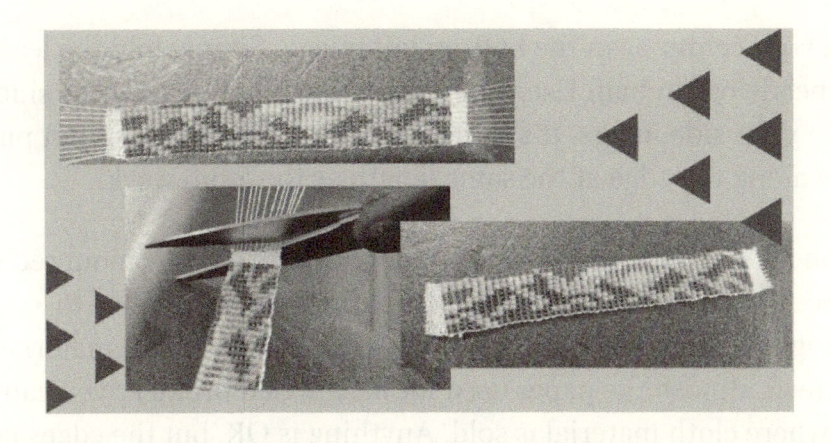

Cut your threads on both ends close to the weaving. You are done with the looming. Congratulations and celebrations! Put on some dancing drums music and dance the Chicken Dance! It's a very special Native American dance the young braves like to dance where they try to look like a chicken. There's another chicken dance that's funny too, but it's not Native American. Look it up online and enjoy some fun; you've earned it. It can't help but ease those muscles and make you feel great!

Now we come to the finishing work. And it is W O R K. Cut a leather strap about an inch wide and however long you need to go around your wrist. Then, add 1 or 1 ½ inches to that length to accommodate the button latch we will be sewing.

Find your center as in the bottom left image. Simply fold the leather and beadwork in half. Use your awl to punch holes along the side as in the right side image. It's rather difficult to see my holes but put them along the edge at the same length as the loom work.

In the image to the right, you can see the loom work is mounted on a piece of material. I like to use something that isn't prone to fraying. For example, a piece of felt is good, or there is a material that feels almost like paper used for backing embroidery you can buy where cloth material is sold. Anything is OK, but the edges need to be hemmed under if they will fray.

I put more glue on the top of my woven places on the ends of the loom work. Beads will not glue down well. They are glass and prone to sliding out of most glues. If you do try to glue the beads themselves, it gets a gooey mess in between your pattern threads and ruins the whole thing. And so, our woven ends we turn under, and the glue is pressed against your material piece. The material should be cut like the above left image, very close to the beading. Only have about ¼ of an inch edge around your actual loomed piece.

Put some glue on the top of the other end, and pull your beadwork somewhat tight to anchor both ends to the material. Aren't you glad we have those woven ends now? These are wonderful to use to glue down your work at either end.

Now you simply tack the material along the edge threads of your beaded work to keep it tight and help remove wrinkles in the beadwork. Loomed beading always tries to wrinkle up when spread out flat.

After you tack around the edges, tie it off and glue this to the middle of your leather strap as in the left image. Line it up with the holes you put in the leather. Now you will simply sew the material to the leather following the beaded work around, using the holes you put in with the awl. You can sew in the middle of your beads to secure the material. It won't be seen after it's done. Hide any knots as you need to by pulling them into the sewed layers before cutting.

Sew it down tightly. It may seem like a lot of work for something so small, but now you will enjoy it for many years. It will be secure. I give a lot of my work away. I certainly don't want it back to have to fix it! That doesn't make a great gift.

Pull out a nice fresh piece of thread. Tie a knot and slide it under the material you sewed your beadwork to. Next, find a handy spot to go into your first row of beads and bring your needle out, as shown in the upper left image. Next, we will begin our edging to absolutely, finally, finish our work.

I chose to use the hot pink for any edging where the sunset is showing. So all along the top, I edged it in hot pink, and all along the bottom, I used dark blue.

You will thread on three beads, jump over and pick up a thread on the edge of your looming. Then, go under it and come back up into that last bead you just put on, as in the lower left image. If you've already done an edging on one of our previous projects, this will now make a lot of sense.

For an edging, you thread on three beads. After those are on, you will thread on two the rest of the way around. You will only need one bead to complete your very last set of edging at the very end.

As you can see, your material has become mostly invisible, and all those ugly knots along the edge of your loom work are simply gone! How nice is that?

Here is your finished work. But now, we will cut a slot for a button to slide through. Pick a button that is mostly flat, and as you attach it, you can add beads inside it like mine if you like. It looks fine without them too. Your slot only needs to be cut like the left middle image as wide as it needs to be to slide your button through. (Be careful not to cut the slit to the end of the leather.)

Chapter Review:

- We learned how to string a loom.
- We learned how to make a pattern and sew our beaded pattern onto the loom.
- Using our beadwork as a bracelet is explained with illustrated steps to finish our work.

Chapter 10: Beaded Flat Work

Hey, we are on the last chapter. If you've done even half of these projects, you will have a great feel for the art of Native American Beading. Now we get to explore the art of Flat Work.

This is named for the fact that you simply bead out a design onto a flat piece of material. It sounds very simple, and it is. However, it's one of the most fun ways to bead because it gives you so much leeway in adding in decorative beads to accentuate your pattern or the way you lay down the beads can be done in a pattern all by itself.

The supplies themselves are simple enough. I have the main white cotton material that I will mount onto my embroidery hoop. This is the base for your Flat Work. I've chosen a very thin piece of leather for a backing, and I want my turtles to be mostly green with yellow flippers.

I saw this design in a Native American pow wow in Spokane, WA. Every year, the Spokane Indians hold their family reunion in the middle of downtown Spokane. Huge tepees are set up with real skins. Drums can be heard all weekend, and the beaded wares are sold along the park's sidewalks, along with buffalo balls on a stick and the famous/infamous fry dough. Fry dough is not the original food of the Native Americans. They were given rations when put on reservations and fry dough developed from that.

I like the three turtles' geometric design and vowed to myself to use it someday, and the day is here. I hope you enjoy sewing it along with me. I always envision these turtles on a log in the middle of a stream or lake like you usually see them. It makes me smile.

To begin, I mount my material to the embroidery hoop. There are two hoops. One fits inside the other, and you lay your material on the smaller one. Then you slide the larger hoop over it to capture the material, screw down the bolt at the top to tighten it, and pull out any wrinkles until the material is quite taut.

I used a medicine bottle to make my circles. It was a small bottle. Then a chapstick bottle to make the inner circles. You can see the pattern is quite easy. Mine is off-kilter in a few places, so I will watch and hope to use the beads to even it out.

Flatwork can be meticulous or just for fun. The process is a lot like all of our beadwork stitches. It's simply one stitch done over and over again.

Look at the image on your left. I pull out some thread about an arm's length and thread on my needle, knotting the bottom ends. Pull it up through your cloth where ever you decide to begin. There is no right or wrong place to start in Flat Work.

You will thread on five beads at a time. If you use more, the beads can become wobbly-looking when tacked down. I have chosen to begin with the line cutting through the back of the turtle. I want this to be a strong point in the pattern. As you thread on the beads, you go behind the middle bead and push back forward, as in the image on the right.

When your needle comes out the front of the work, it's ready to add five more. Coming out of the other beads keeps your beads closely set together, so there are no gaps. You can simply sew on three or four beads, then sew on another few, but you will see the gaps it causes.

From here, you simply sew on the beads in the areas you need to fill. For example, I like to do the outlines first and then fill the center. In this way, they stay more contained and will give a smoother finish.

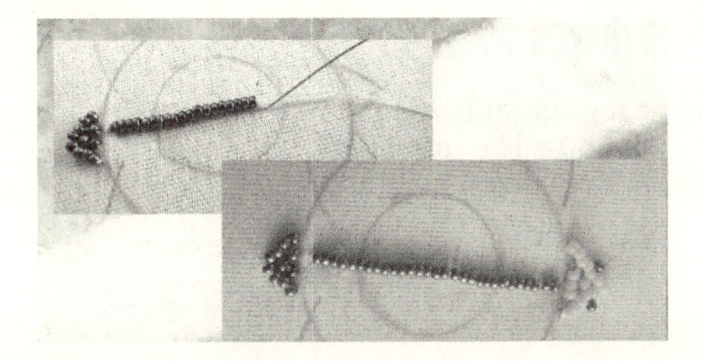

Here is my progress. As you can see in the bottom image, I've left a gap for the outside outline.

I skipped to the middle of my design and put a little bit of pattern in the middle. I changed it up in different directions, so the beads make a statement. You can see my circles wobble a bit around the edges, but they are mostly straight.

Tip #78 - Don't try to cram too many beads into your spaces in your Flat Work pattern.

Keeping your material taunt will help keep spaces opening up between beaded areas. If you need to add beads, it's better to do it at the end than cram them too closely. That will end up where they tend to bulge out in your design.

You will have three layers to your finished turtles:

1. On the top is your beaded work.
2. The middle will be your plastic lid.
3. The bottom is your thin leather piece.

I cut semi-circles out of the plastic lid and the leather. Then, for my top beaded piece, I took out my embroidery hoop and cut it larger with a 1-inch border all the way around.

Glue the back of your beaded work to your plastic lid circular piece. This plastic in the middle of the Flat Work will add stiffness so the work lays flat continually and can be used for several different things.

Tip #79 - Leather car "shammies" work really well when you need a very thin piece of leather to finish your beadwork.

The thin leather is easy to sew through with a regular beading needle and keeps your piece very lightweight.

You can see how I prepare my leather layer in the above images. First, I made small cuts in each end, as in the middle image. The cuts are straight and easy if you fold them like in the image to the left. Then I cut a long strip of about eight inches to thread through the holes in the leather. See the above right image. Have your leather strip lying as flat as possible, not twisted. This is the top of your leather piece.

Take your glue stick and rub glue all over the back of your leather piece—Tuck all the white material under the plastic lid piece in the middle. Next, lay the leather with the glue size on top of that. As you tuck under the white material, the leather side with the glue should catch and hold it. Tuck it a little bit at a time under your plastic lid all around until all the white material is under the plastic and glued and covered by the leather backing.

It's time to finish off our work by sewing all the glued layers together with an edging stitch. I take a fresh piece of thread and slide it on my needle, making a knot with the ends of the thread. If you look at the upper left image, I go into the layers under my beaded work to hide the knot.

Holding the layers together, begin sewing your edging using a larger bead for the edging. My beads in the pattern of this project are size 11, and the edging is a sized 10 dark green bead.

Thread on three beads and jump over about ¼ of an inch. Then, go back up into the last bead you threaded and come out to start over again as in the right image.

The edging stitch pulls the edges of your layers together, makes a nice finished piece to your Flat Work, and keeps the layers from unraveling.

As you go around adding your edging, the first three beads set the edging stitch; then, you switch to two beads each time for the rest of the edge. You will only add one bead to finish the edging stitch at the very end.

Your finished Flat Work should look like the above images. The back side has leather thongs that you can use to attach to a barrette, hat, or anything you might like to adorn. It's very versatile and can be taken off and moved when created this way.

I hope you have enjoyed this project. Any item you may want to depict in a Flat Work design is easily sketched onto a piece of cloth and filled with beads. As I showed you with this stitch, the continual addition of the beads keeps your patterns flowing without gaps along the line of beads.

Tip #80 - Your pattern does not show through when you finish your beading of the Flat Work.

Use lighter colors when sketching onto your cloth, but normally the sketched pattern becomes almost invisible when finished.

Chapter Review:

- We learned how to use an embroidery hoop and sketch a design.
- How to sew beads onto material so that they continually flow and don't leave gaps between the beads is demonstrated.
- Using layers to make our Flat Work versatile to use is shown.
- The edging stitch is explained and illustrated again for finishing our beaded work.

Most Frequently Asked Questions
About Native American Beading

- What is Native American Beading?

    It is the artwork, using beads, of the original tribes inhabiting North America before and after explorers came to hunt and map the new world.

- How do they use the beads in their work?

    The Native Americans used them by sewing beads onto material or leather to adorn moccasins, belts, and almost anything they wore. They have several ways to weave them, looming with beads being the most well-known practice.

- What kind of beads do the Native Americans use?

    The beadwork is predominately done with glass seed beads. However, other types of beads are also used along with the seed beads. For example, semi-precious stone beads are very often used in conjunction with glass ones.

- What colors of beads do Native Americans use?

    Most early Native American beading seemed to lean towards pinks and turquoises for color choices. Yellow was a rare color in the original trade beads. Early beadwork is authenticated by the only yellow beads available at the time, which were a greasy yellow color. Now we see much more variety in color choices. The traditional "fire colors" are used a lot within many tribes. There is a project in this book to give you an example of that.

- Why do the Native Americans do beadwork?

Like all cultures, we adorn ourselves in a variety of ways. Native Americans are the same in their appreciation of beauty. But, in their culture, they also used symbols and figures of animals to tell stories relating to the tribe's history. And it was also a way to distinguish themselves with the financial hierarchy within the tribe.

- What is *regalia*?

This is the traditional Native American form of dress, often using animal hides, feathers, and beautiful beading in bright colors. It's often seen at *pow wows* and within reservations. It tends to be a more formal way of dressing for special occasions or presentations.

Fare Well

Thank you for letting me be your Expert to the world of Native American Beading
I hope it brings you as much joy as it's given me.

About the Author

Leonora Raye, was bequeathed the Native American name, *Little Blue Jay*. She is a direct descendant of the Cherokee tribe. She began beading at the age of six and continues to this day. She has been a part of many Native American beading circles and enjoyed decades of being steeped in the Native American culture.

Many times, the Native Americans are portrayed as a conquered people, but inside the pages of this book, a part of their heritage lives on that will never be conquered. Leonora Raye, or *Little Blue Jay*, has preserved for us a sample of the ingenuity and deftness of her own relatives. The designs and complex stitching are revealed through her willingness to share a lifetime of being a part of Native American Beading.

HowExpert publishes how to guides by everyday experts. Visit HowExpert.com to learn more.

Recommended Resources

- HowExpert.com – Quick 'How To' Guides on All Topics from A to Z by Everyday Experts.
- HowExpert.com/free – Free HowExpert Email Newsletter.
- HowExpert.com/books – HowExpert Books
- HowExpert.com/courses – HowExpert Courses
- HowExpert.com/clothing – HowExpert Clothing
- HowExpert.com/membership – HowExpert Membership Site
- HowExpert.com/affiliates – HowExpert Affiliate Program
- HowExpert.com/jobs – HowExpert Jobs
- HowExpert.com/writers – Write About Your #1 Passion/Knowledge/Expertise & Become a HowExpert Author.
- HowExpert.com/resources – Additional HowExpert Recommended Resources
- YouTube.com/HowExpert – Subscribe to HowExpert YouTube.
- Instagram.com/HowExpert – Follow HowExpert on Instagram.
- Facebook.com/HowExpert – Follow HowExpert on Facebook.
- TikTok.com/@HowExpert – Follow HowExpert on TikTok.

Made in the USA
Las Vegas, NV
04 December 2024